WATERFALLS
of the
Pacific Northwest

One of the many outstanding waterfalls in the Pacific Northwest

back of the hatchery contains some extremely large trout. Food machines are placed around the pond for those interested in feeding the fish and getting a closer look.

Wizard Falls is, in truth, only a mild rapid. Here the river tumbles over a small ledge and into a deep channel, creating the illusion of a bright aqua strip down the center of the river. The best view of this unique feature is from the bridge that leads into the fish hatchery.

Ducks, American dippers, red-winged blackbirds, and Steller's jays can all be seen swimming or darting among the brush along the shore. Also in the area, but rare, are white-headed woodpeckers. Old-growth ponderosa pine covers the canyon walls, and in the spring and early summer months wildflowers abound, including larkspur, monkeyflower, columbine, and lupine.

No trip to the Metolius is complete without a visit to the headwaters located 2 miles from the intersection of US 20 on FS 14. A short 0.25 mile trail leads through the ponderosa pine forest to a low bluff. At its base—and quite literally—springs the Metolius River.

Although Wizard Falls is not a true waterfall, this unique river feature—along with the fish hatchery and the sight of a full-fledged river springing from the base of the Black Butte cinder cone—make it well worth the visit.

WATERFALLS

of the
Pacific Northwest

200+ FALLS
THROUGHOUT OREGON
& WASHINGTON

David L. Anderson

THE COUNTRYMAN PRESS
WOODSTOCK, VERMONT

We welcome your comments and suggestions. Please contact The
Countryman Press, P.O. Box 748, Woodstock, VT 05091, or e-mail
countrymanpress@wwnorton.com.

First Edition

ISBN 978-0-88150-713-3

Cover photo of Lower Proxy Falls (see page 122) and interior photos
by the author
Book design by Deborah Fillion
Page composition by PerfecType, Nashville, TN
Maps by Paul Woodward, © 2007 The Countryman Press

Published by The Countryman Press, P.O. Box 748, Woodstock,
VT 05091

Distributed by W. W. Norton & Company, 500 Fifth Avenue,
New York, NY 10110

Printed in the United States of America

10 9 8 7 6 5 4 3 2 1

To Oliver, Hayley, and Stefanie.

Acknowledgments

I would first like to thank all those people I have met throughout the Pacific Northwest for their kindness, generosity, and willingness to share their local wisdom of the region's spectacular natural wonders. Thanks also to my parents, Louie and Linda Anderson; and to Stefanie Gunderson for her encouragement, and review of the first drafts.

I would like to thank Bill Bowers for his knowledge, patience, and guidance in editing this book. I would also like to extend my appreciation to Jennifer Thompson, Kermit Hummel, and the entire staff at The Countryman Press for all their help.

Contents

Introduction

The intent of this book is not to create a list every of waterfall in the Northwest. In choosing the waterfalls listed here, I attempted to select those which best represent the natural diversity of each region, as well as highlight its natural scenic beauty. The waterfalls have also been grouped so that several waterfalls can be visited in a single outing or over the course of a weekend getaway.

The waterfalls listed in this book vary from roadside vistas to a few more difficult hikes; however, all of the waterfalls are along well-defined trails. I have intentionally left out those which require "bushwhacking" or navigating cross-country. In taking this approach, I have left out a great many waterfalls, some of which are more spectacular than those listed here. For those dedicated individuals intent on hunting down these remote gems, I refer you to the resources listed in this book.

THE PACIFIC NORTHWEST

Prior to the arrival of explorers from Europe, the Native Americans of the Pacific Northwest had developed an extensive trading network along with highly developed salmon-fishing and whale-hunting industries. The numerous tribes of the region had also developed unique and distinct cultures that are still evident in their ceremonial art, elaborate totem poles, and ornately carved canoes and masks.

The first Europeans to visit the region did so by ship. In 1775 the Spanish explorer Don Bruno de Heceta made the first recorded landing on the Washington coast, claiming the lands for Spain. In 1792, the American explorer Capt. Robert Gray further mapped the coastline, discovered the Columbia River, and established an American presence in the region. The British reinforced their claim by sending Capt. George Vancouver, who spent three years in the area, from 1792 to 1794, and produced the most comprehensive survey of the area at the time.

In 1803, President Jefferson won approval from Congress to appropriate funds for a small army unit to explore the Missouri and Columbia

Rivers. The purpose of the expedition was to determine if the Missouri and Columbia Rivers could be used as an efficient trading route by American fur companies in order to compete with British trading companies who were pressing further and further south.

The Corps of Discovery, led by Captains Meriwether Lewis and William Clark, set off from St. Louis in May of 1804. Following the Missouri and Columbia Rivers, the expedition reached the shores of the Pacific Ocean, near the mouth of the Columbia River, in November of 1805. They spent the winter at Fort Clatsop, near present day Astoria, and in March 1806 began their journey home.

While the expedition did not find a trading route, it did spur further exploration. The detailed journals kept by Lewis and Clark contributed important information concerning the land, its native peoples, and the potential riches contained by its natural resources.

It was not until the 1840s that widespread settlement began. Driven by countless reasons—free land, riches, fleeing persecution or economic strife, or just a sense of adventure—nearly 500,000 Americans left their former life behind and headed west along the Oregon Trail. What they found was a land of fertile valleys, towering peaks, endless forests, and a bountiful Pacific Ocean. In part, this influx of Americans forced the British to withdraw their claims to the land. With much of the prime homesteading areas to the south already settled, many later pioneers turned north into the newly opened Washington Territory.

On February 14, 1859, Oregon became the 33rd state of a still-young nation. To the north, people began to settle the Puget Sound. The settlement was accelerated with the completion of the Northern Pacific railroad line in 1873. On November 11, 1889, Washington was welcomed into the union as the 42nd state.

Oregon's 96,000 square miles makes it the 9th largest state in the union, while Washington ranks 18th, with 71,000 square miles. The majority of the region's nearly 10 million residents live in the western valleys along the I-5 corridor in the cities of Seattle, Tacoma, Portland, and Eugene.

For many years, the timber industry dominated the region's economy. More recently, however, this has been replaced by the high-technology, computer software, and electronics industries. Timber is still a large contributor to the economy, along with tourism and farming.

While Oregon has a reputation for rain, Washington actually averages a few more inches per year. Most of the region's annual precipitation falls along the coastline, where in the headlands and coastal mountains it can reach more than 100 inches per year. The rainforests of the Olympic Peninsula can average more than 150 inches. However, east of the Cascades the annual precipitation drops below 30 inches a year, with several towns boasting more than 300 days of sunshine annually.

Although extremes do occur, the climate is generally moderate. Average summer temperatures along the coast are in the 60s and 70s, and in the 50s during the winter. Temperatures in the valleys typically average 5 to 10 degrees warmer. The greatest temperature variations occur east of the Cascades, where summer temperatures can go from near-freezing at night to the upper 80s or 90s in the afternoon.

GEOLOGY

In geological time, the Pacific Northwest is relatively young. Approximately 400 to 300 million years ago the Pacific shore was just off the border of Idaho, and the future state of Oregon consisted of a series of islands just offshore. As the North American continent drifted westward over the Pacific Plate, the islands were lifted, and then joined the North American continent. Evidence of this process can still be seen in the fossil remains of the Palouse and Hells Canyon areas. This same process continues today. Geologic measurements of Cape Blanco indicate that it is rising at a rate of almost 3 inches per 100 years—among the fastest rates in the world.

The Olympic Mountains were formed similarly, as the plate on which they rest inched into the North American Plate 35 million years ago. As the smaller Juan de Fuca plate continued forward, most of it slid beneath the North American Plate. However, some of it was scraped off. As this dome of material grew larger, it began to buckle and fold, giving rise to the Olympic Mountains and their characteristic jumbled appearance.

Between 20 and 15 million years ago, several massive fissures in the earth's crust opened and erupted in a series of basalt lava flows, known as the Columbia River Basalt Lava Flows. These flows traveled as far as 300 miles to reach the Pacific, further extending the coastline and creating many of the headlands we see today, such as Cape Lookout, Tillamook Head, and Cape Meares.

Fueled by the heat of the melting Pacific Plate as it dove beneath the North American continent, the first recognizable peaks of the Cascades began to form a little more than 1 million years ago. Many of these peaks fell dormant, and were heavily eroded by a succession of glaciations.

Others, such as Mount Rainier, Mount St. Helens, Mount Hood, and South Sister remained active, resisting the erosion of the glaciers.

During the last ice age, one of the world's most unique geologic events helped carve the Columbia River Gorge. Near the city of Missoula, Montana, an immense lake formed behind an ice dam. As the water level rose, the dam failed, sending one of the planet's largest floods across the Eastern Washington landscape. The flood waters carved out the potholes of the Palouse, as well as the Washington Coulees, and created an inland sea out of the Willamette Valley. As the flood waters reached the Columbia River Gorge, they scoured it clean, leaving the hanging valleys that form the waterfalls we see in the gorge today.

WATERFALLS

A waterfall is defined as a sudden unsupported drop in a stream. They are created when a stream or river passes over a layer of harder rock to an area of softer, more easily eroded rock. They also occur when the stream or river encounters a plateau, a bluff, or glacier-eroded valley. While the definition seems relatively straightforward, it has given rise to many debates regarding what should be called a waterfall, and determination of waterfall height. For the purposes of this book, I have chosen not to enter the debate. All the entries in the book are considered "waterfalls" regardless of form. I have also used the most commonly published heights for each, and have not attempted to measure them personally.

Although each waterfall is unique, there are certain forms that can be categorized. The following are descriptions of the most common, and the ones used throughout this book.

Cascade: A stream descending over a series of steep steps or rocks in quick succession.

Plunge: A narrow waterfall that has little or no contact with the streambed as it falls.

Curtain: A broad waterfall that has little or no contact with the streambed as it falls.

Fan: A waterfall which begins narrow, then spreads out over the surface it is falling over.

Horsetail: A narrow waterfall that maintains contact with surface it is falling over.

Tiered: A waterfall that makes two or more large drops in quick succession.

Segmented: A waterfall that splits into two or more streams as it falls.

PHOTOGRAPHY

Waterfalls present some unique challenges not often encountered when photographing other subjects. They can be located in remote areas and be difficult to reach. Just by their nature, they are often surrounded by steep cliffs, and getting the composition you've envisioned may be next to impossible. If you can get in close, you may have to deal with spray forming on the lens. Since most waterfalls are set against dark cliffs, surrounded by tall trees, or set in deep canyons and/or gorges, the lighting conditions may make it difficult to obtain a good exposure.

Unfortunately, there is no solution when it comes to where a waterfall may be located. Your only option is to pack as lightly as possible, and put in a little hard work and sweat, in order to reach some of these more remote locations. However, keep in mind that this same isolation may well have saved many of these natural treasures from the pressures of development. Likewise, once you reach the waterfall you may be stuck with the composition that Mother Nature and/or the trail builders have provided. Creative use of a zoom lens may help or, with a little research and a current topographical map, you may be able to find an abandoned road or trail that may lead you to a better view. However, use caution when doing this; trails and roads usually were abandoned for a very good reason.

Exposure and light provide perhaps the greatest challenges to photographing waterfalls. We have all taken photos on a bright, sunny day, only to be disappointed with the results. The vivid colors we originally observed are washed out, and we can not see any detail in the shadows. This disappointment is due to the fact that our eyes are much more sensitive than film or an image sensor. While our eyes are capable of resolving scenes with exposure ranges of seven or eight stops, cameras, both film and digital, are only capable of resolving scenes with an exposure range of four to five stops. In addition, most cameras try to average the overall exposure of a scene. This combination results in details being lost in the shadows, and colors being washed out in the brighter areas of the image.

In order to correct this problem we need to somehow balance the scene. One way of doing this, and probably the most effective one, is to choose when to photograph. An overcast day will provide even illumination as the sunlight filters through the clouds, as long as you remember not to include the sky in the image. Photographing near to sunrise and sunset, or as the sun passes below the nearby horizon, will also help filter the light.

Another way to balance the exposure of a scene is to use a graduated neutral density filter. These are square filters that fade from clear to dark, and attach to the front of the lens with a special adapter. The dark area simply reduces the intensity of the light reaching the film or sensor. The adapter allows you to rotate and slide the filter, in order to place the graduation where you need it in the scene. These filters are particularly useful if you would like to include the sky in your composition.

There are two additional filters you should include in your camera bag. The first is a circular polarizer, a filter that is indispensable for landscape photography. I use a polarizer on perhaps 50 percent of all my images. This filter removes unwanted glare and reflections in the same way as polarized sunglasses. It not only makes the sky bluer and removes surface reflections from water or from wet surfaces, but it also filters reflections from foliage that you may not readily notice without a filter. The effect on your images is to increase color saturation and provide more definition in the shadows.

The second filter is a warming, or an 81-series, filter. These filters have a slight yellow tint, and have the effect of removing the bluish tint that sometimes occurs when photographing in shadows or low light. There are three levels of tint commonly used: 81A, 81B, and 81C, with the 81A having the lightest tint, and the 81C the darkest. When using these filters for photographing waterfalls, it is best to stay with the 81A, since the darker tints tend to make the water look muddy, or unnatural.

Spray can also be another challenge encountered when photographing waterfalls. There are many types of specialty covers and hoods on the market. However, one easy and cheap form of protection is to simply tear a hole in the bottom of a small, white trash bag, and pull the bag over both the lens and camera. With the lens hood on, poke the lens through the hole, and secure the bag with a rubber band. You'll never win a fashion show with this set-up, but it is certainly effective. Keeping spray off the front lens element is a more difficult task, and the only solution I know is to keep the lens cover on until the last moment, and carry plenty of clean, dry lens cloths.

When it comes to composition, there are no rules. After having said that, there are a couple very general guidelines. As a general rule of thumb, small waterfalls are typically photographed with a long shutter speed. This blurs the water and gives it a silky appearance, which emphasizes the delicate nature of the waterfall. Larger waterfalls are typically photographed with short shutter speed, which freezes the motion of the falling water. This helps to project the power and strength of the waterfall. It is also important to keep in mind that many times it is not necessary to include the entire waterfall in the image in order to capture the character of the falls and the surrounding area. A close-up of the base of the falls, in the case of a large waterfall, can project its drama. A close-up of the midsection of a small falls may project a sense of the delicate nature of the stream cascading down the face of a cliff, and hint at the geology that created it. The most important thing to remember about composition, is to photograph what you like and photograph it in the way it appeals to you.

WILDERNESS TRAVEL

Some of the waterfalls described in the book take you into, or through, remote wilderness areas. It is important to remember that emergency facilities in these areas can be limited and cellular phone reception may not be possible.

Depending on what season and region you are traveling in, needs vary greatly. There are, however, several items that are necessities regardless of where you go. These include:

• Extra food such as energy bars or trail mix.
• A small first-aid kit.
• A reliable map and compass.
• A flashlight.
• A blanket.
• A roadside emergency kit.

If you intend to hike some of the longer trails, make sure you have a sturdy, comfortable pair of shoes (preferably hiking boots) and a dry pair of socks. You may also consider bringing some waterproof matches, fire starter, and an extra shirt and/or rain jacket.

If you intend to travel in the higher elevations, remember that the weather can change rapidly and snow is possible in any season.

When traveling in the eastern desert regions you should triple the amount of water you usually carry.

Prior to leaving on any trip it is important to let someone know where you intend to go and when you intend to return.

PRECAUTIONS

Many of the trails pass by pristine streams and lakes and while they may appear pure, every stream is a potential source of the microorganism *Giardia lambli*. *Giardia* is readily spread to surface water through the feces of animals and infected humans. *Giardia* causes severe diarrhea and dehydration.

Poison oak can be found throughout Oregon and Washington and can be identified by its reddish green, oval shaped, and almost oily looking leaves. Poison oak secretes an oily sap that may cause a painful and itchy rash. In more sensitive individuals the rash may produce blisters and a severe burning sensation. If you suspect you have come in contact with poison oak, even with just your clothing, do not touch the affected area. The oil may be spread to other areas. Remove the affected clothing and place it in a plastic bag or wrap it in a towel to keep it away from other items. Thoroughly wash the area affected with a strong soap in cool water. If the irritation continues for an extended period of time or it becomes more severe consult a physician.

Some the trails described in this book bring the reader into wilderness areas populated by mountain lion and black bear. While the probability of having an encounter with a mountain lion is extremely rare it does occur from time to time. In the unlikely event that you do have an encounter the current wisdom is to act as aggressively as possible in order to scare it off. Remain standing, make yourself appear as large as possible, but do not attempt to run. Running may trigger the predatory instinct.

In the rare event that you have an encounter with a black bear you should remain still and avoid eye contact. If the bear should attack, do not fight back and curl into a ball using your hands to protect the back of your neck. As with a mountain lion, do not run since it may trigger the predatory instinct.

Although somewhat rare, rattlesnakes do inhabit the eastern regions of both Oregon and Washington. Care should be taken when stepping over rocks or hidden areas. If you are unfortunate enough to be bitten by a rattlesnake, it is important to stay calm and remember that a bite is rarely fatal. Try to keep the area bitten lower than the heart, and apply a light constricting band about 2" above and below the bite. Seek medical attention as soon as possible.

A PRECIOUS LEGACY

One of the Northwest's most valuable natural resources is its wilderness areas and scenic beauty. It is the responsibility of all individuals who venture into these areas to maintain and protect these natural assets. By following a few basic principles we can help ensure that we protect this precious legacy for the enjoyment of future generations.

Whenever possible walk on pre-existing trails and roads and do not cut across switchbacks.

Pack out all garbage, even if it was left behind by previous visitors.

Don't pick flowers or cut down trees, even dead ones, for use as firewood.

HOW TO USE THIS BOOK

Waterfalls of the Pacific Northwest is organized so it's easy to get all the information you need to take off on the trip of your choice. For each entry there is a listing of basic facts, followed by directions to the waterfall or trailhead, and a detailed description of the waterfall itself.

Trail distances are given in round trip miles and each entry also includes a basic rating of easy, moderate, or difficult. These ratings are based on three factors; the length of the trail, the terrain covered, and the elevation. The basic information also includes a recommendation for the best season to visit the falls. It is based upon such things as when the trail is open, stream flow, and typical weather conditions.

All of the hikes described in the book are on public land or on land owed by organizations such as The Nature Conservancy who grant public access to the trails. All of the trails included in the book are primarily for hiking. None of the hikes permit motorized vehicles. A few of the trails permit mountain bikes and you may be required to share the trail with horses.

Varying rules and regulations apply in the different land management districts and organizations. It is always a good idea to check the rules and regulations before traveling the area.

RESOURCES

National Park Service
www.nps.gov

U.S. Forest Service
www.fs.fed.us

Oregon Parks and Recreation Department
www.prd.state.or.us

Washington State Parks and Recreation Commission
www.parks.wa.gov

U.S. Fish and Wildlife Service
www.fws.gov/refuges

Bureau of Land Management (BLM)
www.blm.gov

America's Byways
www.byways.org

The Nature Conservancy
www.nature.org

Columbia River Gorge National Scenic Area
www.fs.fed.us/r6/columbia/forest

Columbia River Gorge Commission
www.gorgecommission.org

I. Pacific Coast

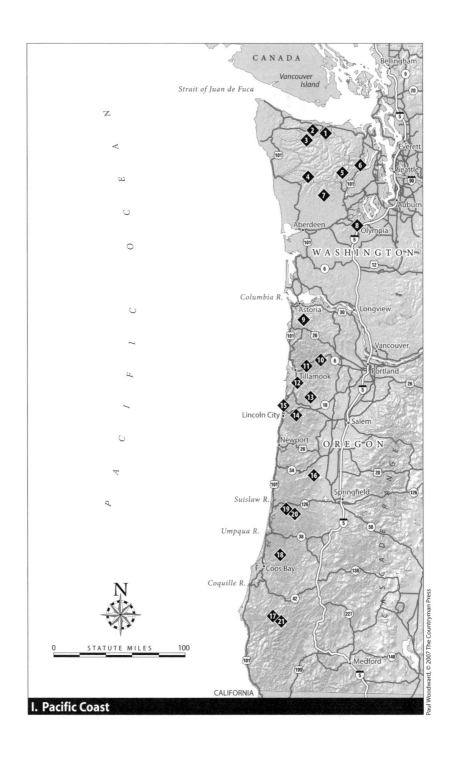

I. Pacific Coast

INTRODUCTION

Unparalleled in its natural beauty, the Pacific Coast offers massive sand dunes, secluded beaches, picturesque lighthouses, and rugged rock headlands. The highly developed Oregon coastline draws million of visitors each year; however, the vast majority rarely deviate from US 101, only getting out of their cars at the designated scenic pullouts and waysides. Even during the peak tourist months of June, July, and August the waterfalls described in this section remain relatively uncrowded.

Although the Washington coastline is much less developed, the majority of its coastal waterfalls lie within, or around, Olympic National Park. Consequently, during the peak tourist season, they can become crowded.

Climate

Not unexpectedly, the coastline is by far the wettest region of the Northwest, with areas at the higher elevations and coastal headlands receiving an annual level of precipitation approaching 100 inches or, in the case of the Olympic rainforest, more than 150 inches. That being said, the majority of this precipitation occurs during the winter months, leaving the summer months relatively dry. Temperatures are moderate throughout the year, with winter temperatures in the 50s or 60s, and summer temperatures in the 60s or 70s. Morning fog is a frequent visitor along the coastline during the summer months, but usually burns off by the late morning or early afternoon.

Precautions

Before you venture out onto the beach or into tidal pools, check the local tide tables. Incoming tides can rapidly isolate rocks from headlands and the shore, stranding unsuspecting hikers. Avoid the temptation of strolling out to an interesting rock without knowing when the tide will roll back in. Free tide tables are available at all state park offices, information centers, and at many shops and motels.

Always keep an eye on the ocean. "Sneaker" waves, unusually large and powerful waves, can appear without warning, even on calm days, and are impossible to predict.

Take care when wading along the beach. Strong currents and undertows are common, and can quickly sweep unwary beachcombers and waders off their feet and out to sea.

Driftwood is common along the shoreline. Many of these logs are waterlogged and weigh several tons, easily crushing an individual. Avoid climbing on driftwood stacks, or even individual logs.

Attractions

- The San Juan Island National Historic Park is located on San Juan Island and can be reached by ferry. The park is a reminder of the sometimes fierce competition between the U.S. and Great Britain to gain control of the Pacific Northwest. Here, in 1859, the U.S. and Britain squared off in a remarkable dispute over a dead British pig. Today the island is a mecca for bicyclists traveling the roads, hikers exploring the woodland trails, and kayakers paddling the saltwater shore, hoping for glimpses of orcas, also known as killer whales.

- Olympic National Park is located in the northwest corner of Washington. The park encompasses rugged glaciated peaks, a temperate rainforest with Sitka spruce blanketed in moss, sandy ocean beaches, and rocky tide pools. Roads provide access to the beaches and spring wildflowers of Hurricane Ridge, but the interior of the park remains a wilderness open only to hikers.

- Stretching from Long Beach in Washington to Cannon Beach in Oregon are the 12 sites that make up the Lewis and Clark National Historic Park. On the Washington side of the Columbia River, the interpretive center at Cape Disappointment State Park offers exhibits pertaining to the heritage of the area. In Oregon, Fort Clatsop provides a look into the lives of these explorers, through reenactments and a replica of the actual fort that housed the Corps of Discovery during the winter of 1805 and 1806.

- In 1970, in order to protect colonies of nesting seabirds and mammals, Congress designated all of Oregon's coastal islands and sea stacks off-limits to public access, thus creating the Oregon Islands Wilderness Area. While direct access is prohibited, there are many places along the coast to observe nesting activity. These include Samuel H. Boardman State Park, Cape Sebastian, Cape Blanco, Coquille Point, Heceta Head, Cape Perpetua, Seal Rock, Yaquina Head, Cascade Head, Cape Meares, and Ecola State Park.

- The Yaquina Head Outstanding Natural Area is located 3 miles north of Newport, and is home to the Yaquina Head Lighthouse. The lighthouse was built in 1872 and stands 93 feet high, making it Oregon's tallest lighthouse. The lighthouse is open for tours from 9 AM to 4 PM daily during the summer, and noon to 4 PM during the winter. Yaquina Head also offers an interpretive center that explores the geological, cultural, and natural history of the area. Two tide pool areas, a cobble beach and the all-accessible quarry tide pool, offer the opportunity to observe local intratidal sea life. A viewing point next to the lighthouse also provides an eye-level view of nesting seabirds on the rocks (Oregon Islands Wilderness Area) just offshore.

- Located near the south end of Newport's historic Yaquina Bay Bridge is the Oregon Coast Aquarium. Once home to the killer whale movie star Keiko, the tank in which he was once housed has been converted into a dramatic exhibit where visitors pass through a submerged 200-foot acrylic tunnel while large sharks and rays pass both above and below. Other exhibits include a large seabird aviary, sea otters, seals and sea lions, jellyfish, and others exploring the various aspects of Oregon's coastal ecosystem.

- The Oregon Dunes Overlook is located 10 miles north of Reedsport, and offers the opportunity to glimpse a portion of the largest expanse of costal sand dunes in North America. The Oregon Dunes National Recreation Area extends 40 miles along the coastline, from the town of Florence to Coos Bay. Formed by both wind and water, some of the largest dunes can reach a height of 500 feet and extend for more than a mile in length. Several hiking options exist within the Recreation Area. For more information stop by the Oregon Dunes NRA Visitor Center, located in Reedsport, which also includes natural and cultural history exhibits.

MADISON CREEK FALLS

Location: Olympic National Park
Maps: USGS–Elwaha
Stream: Madison Creek
Round Trip Hike Distance: 0.25 mile

Difficulty: Easy
Height: 80 feet
Volume: Small
Best Season: Winter, spring, summer, fall

SPECIAL NOTES: A National Park entrance fee is required and can be paid at the park entrance station. The trail is paved and wheelchair accessible.

DIRECTIONS: From Port Angeles, travel west 9 miles on US 101 to

Madison Creek Falls

Hot Springs Road. Turn left and follow Hot Springs Road 2 miles to the National Park Entrance station.

THE FALLS: The trail begins at the parking area next to the entrance station, and wanders through a meadow and a mixed grove of oak and Douglas fir. It then joins Madison Creek and follows it into a small dell, where Madison Creek slides 80 feet down a moss-covered basalt cliff and into a small shallow pool. During periods of moderately high flow, small rivulets extend from the main cascade, providing a very picturesque scene. Since the falls face west, the best light is usually near sunset. A warming filter and polarizer are helpful in bringing out the greens of the moss.

2

MARYMERE FALLS

Location: Olympic National Park
Maps: USGS–Lake Crescent
Stream: Falls Creek
Round Trip Hike Distance: 1.5 miles

Difficulty: Easy
Height: 90 feet
Volume: Small
Best Season: Winter, spring, fall

SPECIAL NOTES: No fees or permits are required. The trail is wheelchair accessible to Barnes Creek. This is one of the most popular trails in Olympic National Park, and during the summer months it can become very crowded.

DIRECTIONS: Follow US 101 west 22 miles, from Port Angeles to the Storm King Ranger Station on the shores of Lake Crescent.

THE FALLS: The trail begins at the parking area and leads through a short tunnel which passes under US 101. From here, the mostly level gravel path leads through old-growth Douglas fir, cedar, and spruce draped in moss. You soon reach the fern-lined Barnes Creek, where the trail runs parallel to it for a few hundred yards before crossing it on a half-log footbridge. The creek was named for the

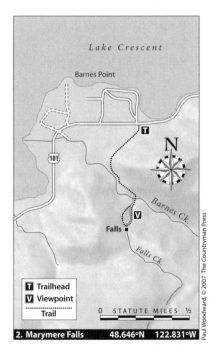

Barnes family, who were early homesteaders in the area, and the waterfall was named for Mary Barnes.

Continuing along for a short distance, a second footbridge crosses Falls Creek just before a trail junction, which is just the start of a small loop with several viewpoints halfway up the falls. Choose the lower "easy" route, which will first bring you to the lower viewpoint at the base of the 90-foot-high falls, before continuing to the upper viewpoints.

The best view of the entire waterfall is from the lower viewpoint. The waterfall first freefalls for 40 feet in a thin ribbon, before crashing against the moss- and fern-covered basalt cliff, and tumbling the remaining 50 feet into a small plunge pool at the fall's base. Although the upper viewpoints don't provide the best views, they do provide a refreshing mist after the moderately strenuous climb.

3

SOL DUC FALLS

Location: Olympic National Park

Maps: USGS–Bogachiel Peak

Stream: Sol Duc River

Round Trip Hike Distance: 2.25 miles

Difficulty: Easy

Height: 40 feet

Volume: Medium

Best Season: Spring, summer, fall, winter

SPECIAL NOTES: An entrance fee to the National Park is required. This trail can become very crowded in the peak summer tourist season.

DIRECTIONS: From the small resort area of Fairholm, located on the far west end of Lake Crescent, travel south on US 101 for 1.75 miles to the well marked Sol Duc Road. Turn left and follow the road 13.5 miles, passing the Sol Duc Hot Springs, to its end at the trailhead.

THE FALLS: A coffee kiosk at the trailhead testifies to the popularity of this trail. From the parking area, the trail sets off through old-growth Douglas fir, hemlock, and cedar draped in moss. A thick undergrowth of sword and bracken ferns, rhododendron, and Oregon-grape reminds you that even though you are in the Pacific Northwest, you are also in the heart of a rainforest.

The mostly level trail continues along, crossing a few small and seasonal

Sol Duc Falls

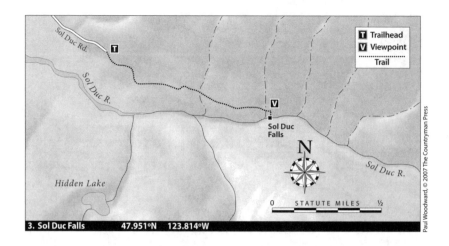

3. Sol Duc Falls   47.951°N   123.814°W

streams, until you begin to hear the roar of the falls. At the junction, follow the trail to the left, passing an old log shelter, as it descends to the bridge over the gorge just downstream from the waterfall. When the Sol Duc is running at an average flow, the river is split into three segments before plunging into a narrow gorge, where the turbulent waters then tumble into a deep-green pool. The view from the bridge offers the best view of the falls, and down into the narrow gorge. Another railed viewpoint at the head of the falls lets you feel the spray and offers good views of just the falls. Sol Duc is a native phrase meaning "sparkling waters."

This is one of the most photographed waterfalls in the Northwest, so getting a new perspective is nearly impossible. The best light is in the morning, before the sun rises above the tree line. This will also better allow you to photograph from the bridge since most visitors arrive later on in the day, and the bridge tends to shake with several people walking on it. A polarizer and warming filter are recommended.

On your way back from hiking to the falls, stop by and visit the Sol Duc Hot Springs located just 1.5 miles back down the road. A native legend tells of the creation of Sol Duc Hot Springs and nearby Olympic Hot Springs on a tributary of the Elwha River. Two dragon-like creatures (Sol Duc and Elwha) engaged in a mighty and desperate battle. There was no victor and both admitted defeat. Each of the creatures crawled back into their separate caves, where they still weep hot tears of disgrace.

4

MERRIMAN FALLS

Location: Olympic National Forest
Maps: USGS–Lake Quinault
Stream: Merriman Creek
Round Trip Hike Distance: At roadside

Difficulty: Easy
Height: 40 feet
Volume: Small
Best Season: Winter, spring, fall

SPECIAL NOTES: No fees or permits are required.

DIRECTIONS: From Lake Quinault, follow South Shore Road 3.5 miles, past the Gatton Creek Campground, to a large unmarked turnout next to the bridge crossing Merriman Creek.

THE FALLS: Merriman Creek horsetails 40 feet down a moss- and fern-covered basalt wall before splashing onto the jumble of rocks and logs below. As you might expect, being nestled in the heart of the rainforest, everything is covered in moss and ferns. Usually a jumble of debris in the stream distracts from the overall scene of a waterfall, but here it adds an almost mystical feel.

Although there is no true trail, access to the falls from the roadside pullout is easy and many different angles of the falls are possible. Photographers will find a polarizing and warming filter are extremely useful.

5

HAMMA HAMMA FALLS

Location: Hamma Hamma Recreation Area
Maps: USGS–Mt. Skokomish
Stream: Hamma Hamma River
Round Trip Hike Distance: At roadside

Difficulty: Easy
Height: 70 feet
Volume: Medium
Best Season: Spring, summer, fall

SPECIAL NOTES: No fees or permits are required.

DIRECTIONS: From Hoodsport follow US 101 north to Hamma Hamma Road. Turn left onto Hamma Hamma Road, and follow it for 6.5 miles and then turn right at the junction following the Lena Creek signs. Continue for another 7 miles to the bridge crossing the Hamma Hamma River, located just above the falls.

THE FALLS: Pull to the side of the road and walk back along the road to the bridge, where you will have a dizzying view looking straight down onto the falls. The bridge marks the end of the road, so there is no problem with traffic or parking. Here the Hamma Hamma (a Native American term for "stinky") has carved out a narrow gorge, where the two-tiered, 70-foot-high waterfall is nestled. The first tier drops 10 feet into a very turbulent pool, just before the main tier drops another 60 feet into a large deep-green pool. It is possible to get a better view of the falls from near the bottom by scrambling down the rough, but well-defined, trail near the end of the bridge.

This is a very scenic and, under the right lighting conditions, very photogenic waterfall. Since the falls face east, the best light is early in the morning. Some interesting images can be achieved from the bridge using a telephoto lens. However, the best views require you to make the scramble to the base.

6

ROCKY BROOK FALLS

Location: Olympic National Forest **Difficulty:** Easy
Maps: USGS–Brinnon **Height:** 120 feet
Stream: Rocky Brook **Volume:** Small
Round Trip Hike Distance: 0.12 **Best Season:** Winter, spring, fall
mile

SPECIAL NOTES: No fees or permits are required. During the summer months the flow is dramatically reduced.

DIRECTIONS: From the small town of Brinnon, drive 1 mile west on US 101 to Dosewallips Road. Turn left onto Dosewallips Road and follow it 3 miles to the Rocky Brook Bridge, and park at the turnout on the far side of the bridge.

THE FALLS: From the turnout, follow the well-defined path past the power station, where you soon come to the rocky base of the 120-foot-high falls. The waters of Rocky Brook cascade down the large rock cliff and into a large plunge pool at its base. The falls fan out near the base, with several rivulets extending from the main stream, making it very photogenic.

The waterfall faces southeast so the best light is in the early morning. A wide-angle lens along with a polarizing filter and graduated neutral density filter are helpful.

7

SPOON CREEK FALLS

Location: Olympic National Forest
Maps: USGS–Grisdale
Stream: Spoon Creek
Round Trip Hike Distance: 0.5 mile

Difficulty: Easy
Height: 60 feet
Volume: Small
Best Season: Winter, spring, summer, fall

SPECIAL NOTES: A Northwest Forest Pass is required to park at the trailhead, and is available at ranger stations and from many private vendors.

DIRECTIONS: From Montesano, travel 1 mile west on US 12 to Wynoochee Road (Devonshire Road) and turn right. Follow Wynoochee Road, which soon becomes FS 22, 34 miles to FS 23. Turn right onto FS 23, and follow it 3 miles to the trailhead just past Spoon Creek.

THE FALLS: The trail leads 100 feet from the small parking area, through cedar and

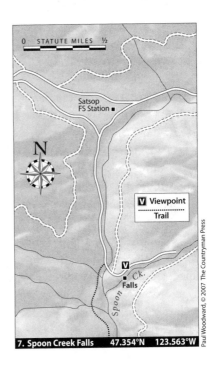

hemlock, to the upper viewpoint. From here, you can peer into the small gorge that Spoon Creek has carved out and see the upper two small cascades just before the main falls. It also allows you to survey the large, deep plunge pool just below the base of the falls. From here the trail leads down, sometimes steeply, another 0.25 mile to the creek. However, in order to view the falls, you need to walk back up the creek 50 to 100 feet, where you can view the falls across the plunge pool.

The falls face southwest, so the late afternoon hours are the best time to photograph. Here the use of a polarizer is essential.

8

TUMWATER FALLS

Location: Tumwater Falls Park
Maps: USGS–Tumwater
Stream: Deschutes River
Round Trip Hike Distance: 0.25 mile

Difficulty: Easy
Height: 30 feet
Volume: Large
Best Season: Winter, spring, summer, fall

SPECIAL NOTES: No fees or permits are required. The trail is wheelchair accessible.

DIRECTIONS: The waterfall is located in the city of Olympia, alongside I-5. From I-5, take Exit 103, and follow the signs to Tumwater Park on East Bay Drive.

THE FALLS: This waterfall has a long history. It was originally named Puget Sound Falls by the early settlers in the area, but was changed to Chutes River Falls in 1841 by representatives of the Hudson's Bay Company. The native Chinook, meanwhile, called the river "Tumtum," the term they used for rushing water, because it reminded them of the sound of a beating heart. In 1845, a party of American settlers arrived and, borrowing from the Chinook, coined the term Tumwater. The waterfall gained fame when the nearby Olympia brewery, now closed, used its image on their label.

The trail from the park leads across a bridge just above the waterfall, and down to a concrete viewing platform just below the falls. The

30-foot-high waterfall has two segments, but only one is visible from the platform. The best views of the waterfall are from, or near, the bridge.

There are two much-smaller waterfalls—Upper Tumwater Falls and Middle Tumwater Falls—which can both be viewed by following the trail paralleling the river.

9

YOUNGS RIVER FALLS

Location: Youngs River Falls State Park
Maps: USGS–Olney
Stream: Youngs River
Round Trip Hike Distance: At roadside
Height: 60 feet
Volume: Large
Best Season: Spring, summer, fall, winter

SPECIAL NOTES: No fees or permits are required. A popular local swimming location, the falls can become crowded during summer weekends.

DIRECTIONS: From Astoria, follow OR 202 south for 10 miles toward the small town of Olney. Follow the Youngs River sign and after approximately 4 miles, you cross the Youngs River. Just past the bridge, an unmarked road takes you a few hundred yards to the parking area.

THE FALLS: A waterfall seems like the last thing you should be looking for as you drive along the tidal flats and estuary of Youngs Bay. However, as you drive the last few yards to the falls, the placid Youngs River rapidly changes its demeanor as it cascades 60 feet down a small basalt bluff.

Located just a few miles from Fort Clatsop, it's not surprising that the first Europeans to discover the falls were a small hunting party from the Lewis and Clark expedition. On March 1 of 1806, Corps of Discovery member Sergeant Patrick Gass wrote in his journal, "our hunters discovered falls, which had about 60 feet of a perpendicular pitch." Since then the falls has become a favorite local swimming location, and the waterfall has been featured in several movies and commercials. A short trail leads from the parking area down to the rocky beach, and the best views of the waterfall.

10

UNIVERSITY FALLS

Location: Tillamook State Forest
Maps: USGS–Woods Point
Stream: Elliot Creek
Round Trip Hike Distance: 1 mile

Difficulty: Easy
Height: 80 feet
Volume: Small
Best Season: Spring, fall

SPECIAL NOTES: No fees or permits are required. The waterfall is located in a popular ATV area. Use caution when driving to the trailhead.

DIRECTIONS: From Portland, drive 41 miles west on US 6 to the Coast Range summit near milepost 33. Turn left onto Saddle Mountain Road, which almost immediately turns to gravel. Follow the road for 3.5 miles, following the signs and keeping right at the first fork and left at the second. A small, signed pullout marks the trailhead.

THE FALLS: From the parking area the trail heads up a few hundred feet, and crosses a dirt logging road before gradually heading back down toward Elliot Creek. The trail passes through second-growth Douglas fir and alder, and past the rapidly decaying remains of the Tillamook Burns. This area was once struck by what the locals called the six-year curse, beginning in 1933. A series of devastating forest fires burned hundreds of thousands of acres of forest in 1933, 1939, and yet again in 1945.

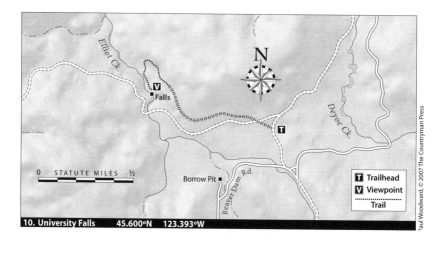

As you reach the creek, continue upstream a few hundred yards to the base of the 80-foot-high fan of University Falls, as it cascades down the jagged rock face. The late-afternoon hours provide the best light to photograph the waterfall. In the fall, make sure to include the yellow leaves of the surrounding alder trees in your composition.

11

BRIDGE CREEK FALLS

Location: Tillamook State Forest
Maps: USGS–Jordan Creek
Stream: Bridge Creek
Round Trip Hike Distance: 0.12 mile

Difficulty: Easy
Height: 50 feet
Volume: Small
Best Season: Spring, fall

SPECIAL NOTES: No fees or access permits are required.

DIRECTIONS: From Tillamook, drive 19.75 miles east on US 6, to a large turnout on the right side of the road.

THE FALLS: From the pullout a short trail leads up along the creek, lined with alder, vine maple, and ferns. Along the way the trail passes over several series of stone stairs on its way to the base of the first tier of the 50-foot-high, two-tiered horsetail. Bridge Creek first slides 30 feet down a moss-covered rock face, and into a small channel, before cascading the remaining 20 feet over a jumble of moss-covered rocks.

Although the area is relatively open, the falls face north and are situated in a small shallow canyon, so the best light for photographing is in the morning or late afternoon. The best views are from the trail just below the second tier and at the base of the first tier, where you can concentrate on the water as it tumbles down the moss-covered rock face.

12

MUNSON CREEK FALLS

Location: Munson Creek State
Natural Site, Tillamook State Forest
Maps: USGS–Beaver
Stream: Munson Creek
Round Trip Hike Distance: 0.75
mile
Difficulty: Easy
Height: 266 feet
Volume: Medium
Best Season: Early spring, late fall

SPECIAL NOTES: No permits or fees are required. This enjoyable stroll through old-growth cedar, alder, and maple and along Munson Creek is tucked just far enough off busy US 101 to avoid the summer crowds.

DIRECTIONS: From Tillamook, travel south on US 101 for 8 miles, and turn left on Munson Creek Road. A small sign along US 101 also points the way. After approximately 0.5 mile, the road turns to gravel. Follow the park signs another mile to Munson Creek State Park, which will be to your right.

THE FALLS: The wide and well-maintained trail begins at the top end of the park turnaround. The trail follows the creek through large cedar, alder, and maple covered in moss. After 0.25 mile, the trail ends at the falls viewpoint. At 266 feet, Munson Creek Falls is the tallest waterfall in the Coast Range. The creek on which the falls is located is named after Gorgan Munson, an early settler of the area.

The waterfall is at its highest flow in the spring and winter. In the late spring and early fall, the view of the lower portion of the falls is obscured by the alder, bigleaf, and vine maple.

The basalt rock cliff that creates the falls was originally the seafloor of the Pacific Ocean. It was created by undersea eruptions 15 to 20 million years ago, during the Miocene Period. Due to the action of the Continental Plate passing over the Pacific Plate, it has exposed the ancient seafloor.

Munson Creek Falls

13

PHEASANT FALLS AND NIAGARA FALLS

Location: Siuslaw National Forest

Maps: USGS–Pheasant Creek

Stream: Pheasant Creek

Round Trip Hike Distance: 2 miles

Difficulty: Moderate

Height: Pheasant Falls, 100 feet; Niagra Falls, 140 feet

Volume: Small

Best Season: Spring, fall, winter

SPECIAL NOTES: No fees or permits are required. Two 100-foot-high waterfalls spill into Pheasant Creek's secluded box canyon. An easy 1-mile path descends along Pheasant Creek to viewpoints at the fall's base.

DIRECTIONS: From Tillamook, drive south along US 101 approximately 15 miles to the small town of Beaver. Turn left onto the Blaine-Nestucca River Road and follow it for 6.5 miles to the small farming community of Blaine. Stay to the right and after another 4.5 miles turn right onto a narrow paved FS 8533 and follow the Niagara Falls Trail signs. Follow the main road straight for 4.25 miles and turn right just past a small TRAIL sign. Another 0.75 mile brings you to the parking area on the left.

THE FALLS: From the parking area, the trail leads downhill toward

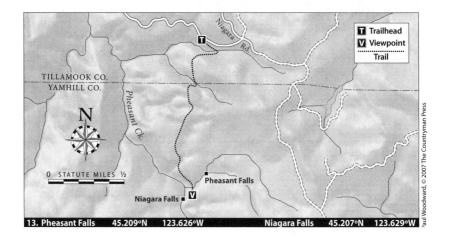

Trailhead	T
Viewpoint	V
Trail	

TILLAMOOK CO.
YAMHILL CO.

Niagara Rd.

Pheasant Ck.

N

0   STATUTE MILES   ½

Pheasant Falls

Niagara Falls   V

13. Pheasant Falls   45.209°N   123.626°W   Niagara Falls   45.207°N   123.629°W

Paul Woodward, © 2007 The Countryman Press

the creek, through tall Douglas fir with an understory of salal and vine maple. Spring brings big three-petaled trillium, the five-petaled candy flower, and delicately belled stalks of wild lily-of-the-valley. Look for yellow monkeyflower on the banks of the creek.

The trail continues to meander along the creek, crossing it several times, before reaching the base of the 100-foot-high Pheasant Falls as it fans out and cascades down the rocky cliff face. Continuing on for another 100 yards will bring you to a small picnic area, with a view of the 140-foot-high Niagara Falls. From here you can watch the waters of Pheasant Creek as they plummet off the rim of the basalt cliff. On your way back, look for yellow monkeyflower and skunk cabbage along the creek, and more trillium peeking from beneath Douglas fir.

14

DRIFT CREEK FALLS

Location: Siuslaw National Forest
Maps: USGS–Drift Creek
Stream: Drift Creek
Round Trip Hike Distance: 3 miles

Difficulty: Moderate
Height: 75 feet
Volume: Small
Best Season: Spring, summer, fall, winter

SPECIAL NOTES: A Northwest Forest Pass is required to park at the trailhead, and is available at ranger stations and many private vendors.

The highlight of this trail is the suspension bridge that crosses 100 feet above the creek, just above Drift Creek Falls. Even during the summer months portions of the trail can be muddy.

DIRECTIONS: From Portland, follow US 18 west toward Lincoln City. Five miles before reaching US 101, turn left onto Bear Creek Road (Forest Service Road 17). Continue on Bear Creek Road for 3.5 miles, where it turns into FS 17. Continue straight on this road for another 7 miles to the paved parking area on the right. From Lincoln City, travel east on US 18 for 5 miles until you reach Bear Creek Road on your right.

THE FALLS: The well-maintained trail begins with a gradual descent through a dense forest of Douglas fir and hemlock on its way down to the creek. Sword and bracken fern, along with vine maple and salal, make

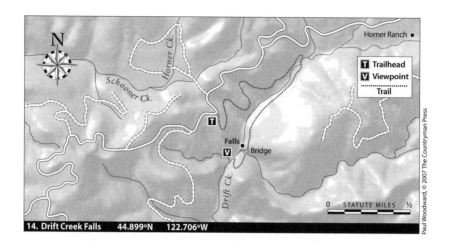

up the majority of the understory. Early spring also brings blooming trillium. After 0.75 mile, the trail skirts by a clear-cut before entering an old-growth forest of hemlock, fir, and red cedar. If you are hiking the trail close to sunset, you may get a glimpse of a spotted owl, a species which has been the source of much controversy in the Pacific Northwest. The old-growth forest of the Drift Creek Wilderness Area has the largest population of spotted owls in the Coast Range.

The trail crosses the creek at the 1-mile mark. A quarter mile farther brings you to the edge of the Drift Creek Canyon, and the magnificent suspension bridge. The bridge was completed in 1997, and is dedicated to Scott Paul, who lost his life on the project. The bridge is 240 feet in length, only 30 inches wide, and crosses 100 feet above Drift Creek. While it may look delicate, the bridge is strong enough to support 80 tons!

A small picnic area on the opposite side is a nice place to rest and have lunch. The trail continues on for another 0.25 mile down to the creek bank, and the best view of the falls with the bridge hovering above. The falls itself is a thin ribbon, 75 feet high.

Drift Creek Falls

15

CHITWOOD FALLS

Location: Cascade Head Nature
Preserve
Maps: USGS–Cascade Head
Stream: Chitwood Creek
Round Trip Hike Distance: 5.5

miles
Difficulty: Moderate
Height: 140 feet
Volume: Small
Best Season: Summer, fall

SPECIAL NOTES: No fees or permits are required; however, a donation is suggested. The trail passes through property owned by The Nature Conservancy, and is closed from January 1 to July 15 in order to help protect native wildflowers, and the highly endangered Oregon silverspot butterfly.

DIRECTIONS: From Lincoln City, follow US 101 north 4 miles to the gravel Cascade Head Road (FS 1861). Turn left onto Cascade Head Road, and follow the HART'S COVE signs for 4 miles, to the parking lot at the road's end.

THE FALLS: Cascade Head was named by passing sailors for the many cascades that flow down its cliffs and into the Pacific. The property is now part of The Nature Conservancy's Cascade Head Nature Preserve.

From the parking area the path meanders through a large hemlock grove for approximately 0.75 mile where the trail comes to a wooden footbridge crossing Cliff Creek. Continuing on, Sitka spruce appear more

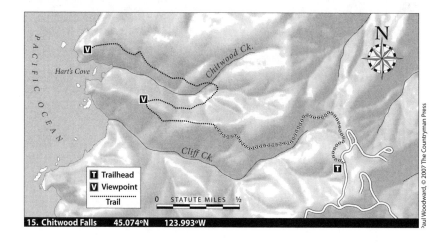

frequently, while below, salal mixed with trillium and fairy belles grow, adding a splash of color in the spring. After 2.75 miles, the trail encounters a small footbridge leading across Chitwood Creek. Another 0.5 mile, and the trail comes to the meadow that was once part of the Taggard homestead. Follow the path to the left where after another 0.25 mile brings you to the viewpoint overlooking Hart's Cove, and the thin, 140-foot-high, ribbon of Chitwood Falls, as it plunges into the Pacific.

16

ALSEA FALLS AND GREEN PEAK FALLS

Location: Alsea Falls Recreation Site
Maps: USGS–Glenbrook
Stream: Alsea River (South Fork), Peak Creek
Round Trip Hike Distance: 200 yards Alsea Falls; 0.75 mile Green

Peak Falls
Difficulty: Easy
Height: 30 feet, Alsea Falls; 60 feet, Green Peak Falls
Volume: Medium
Best Season: Spring, summer, fall, winter

SPECIAL NOTES: No fees or permits are required. Poison oak is abundant, so use caution if you venture off the trail.

DIRECTIONS: From Corvallis, travel west on OR 34 to the small town of Alsea. From Alsea, continue south for 1 mile, following the Alsea Falls signs, to South Fork Road. Turn left, and follow South Fork Road 8.5 miles to the well-marked Alsea Falls picnic area.

THE FALLS: Alsea Falls is located just downstream of the Alsea Falls picnic area. A small

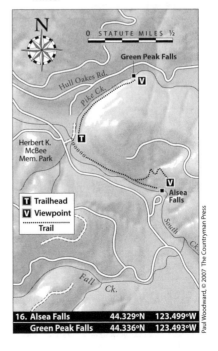

N

0 STATUTE MILES ½

Green Peak Falls

Hull Oakes Rd.

Pike Ck.

Herbert K. McBee Mem. Park

T Trailhead
V Viewpoint
.... Trail

South Ck.

Alsea Falls

Fall Ck.

| 16. Alsea Falls | 44.329°N | 123.499°W |
| Green Peak Falls | 44.336°N | 123.493°W |

Paul Woodward, © 2007 The Countryman Press

viewpoint at the far end of the picnic area overlooks the 30-foot-high slide. In order to reach the best view of the falls, continue straight down the well-maintained path through oak and maple trees to the base of the falls and the deep plunge pool.

Green Peak Falls can be reached by either driving or walking up South Fork Road 0.75 mile to the privately owned Hubert K. McBee Memorial Park. From the picnic area, follow the dirt path along Pike Creek and through old-growth Douglas fir and hemlock to the viewpoint overlooking the 60-foot-high tiered falls as it cascades 50 feet down the rocky cliff face and then makes another short 5-foot drop. A short but very steep trail leads down to the small plunge pool.

17

ELK CREEK FALLS

Location: Siskiyou National Forest

Maps: USGS–Eden Valley

Stream: Elk Creek

Round Trip Hike Distance: 0.25 mile

Difficulty: Easy

Height: 120 feet

Volume: Small

Best Season: Spring, fall

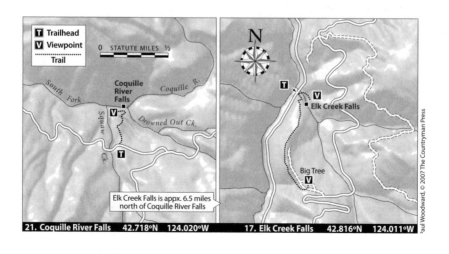

Trailhead
Viewpoint
Trail

0 STATUTE MILES ½

South Fork

Coquille River Falls

Coquille R.

Squaw Ck.

Drowned Out Ck.

Elk Creek Falls is appx. 6.5 miles north of Coquille River Falls

N

Elk Creek Falls

Big Tree

21. Coquille River Falls   42.718°N   124.020°W

17. Elk Creek Falls   42.816°N   124.011°W

Paul Woodward. © 2007 The Countryman Press

SPECIAL NOTES: No fees or permits are required.

DIRECTIONS: From Roseburg, travel west on US 42 to South Fork Coquille River Road, located 3 miles east of Myrtle Point. Turn south and follow it 27 miles, through Powers and toward Agness, to the well-marked Elk Creek Falls pullout.

THE FALLS: A short path leads from the pullout to the 120-foot-high falls. The waters of Elk Creek tumble over a rocky bluff, and into a rocky grotto lined by alder and sword fern. The fall is best viewed in the spring or fall; it is reduced to a trickle by the end of summer.

If you would like to stretch your legs a bit more, follow the right fork of the path from the pullout. This trail switchbacks up the ridge through Douglas fir, maple, and rhododendron to a small picnic area and "Big Tree"—a 239-foot-high, 12-foot-thick Port Orford cedar, the world's largest.

18

GOLDEN FALLS AND SILVER FALLS

Location: Golden and Silver Falls State Natural Area

Maps: USGS–Golden Falls

Stream: Glenn Creek, Silver Creek

Round Trip Hike Distance: Golden Falls, 0.5 mile;

Silver Falls, 1 mile

Difficulty: Easy

Height: Golden Falls, 200 feet; Silver Falls, 160 feet

Volume: Medium

Best Season: Spring, summer, fall, winter

SPECIAL NOTES: No fees or permits are required. The trail to the top of Golden Falls is not recommended for small children.

DIRECTIONS: From the town of Coos Bay, follow US 101 south 3 miles to Eastside Road and turn left, following the signs for Coos River and Golden and Silver Falls State Recreation Area. Follow the road 24 miles, through the small town of Allegany, to its end at Golden and Silver Falls State Recreation Area.

THE FALLS: Beginning at the parking area, cross Silver Creek on the small footbridge and turn right at the fork. The path leads 0.25 mile, through a grove of large myrtlewood trees, to its end at the viewpoint at the base of Golden Falls. Here, the waters of Glenn Creek tumble and slide down the 200-foot-high rock face.

The falls draws its name from Dr. C. B. Golden, who was the first Grand Chancellor of the Oregon Knights of Pythias.

To reach Silver Falls, take the left fork at the footbridge, and follow the path up through Douglas fir, sword fern, and rhododendron for 0.5 mile, where a short trail spur to the left leads to the base of Silver Falls. During pe-

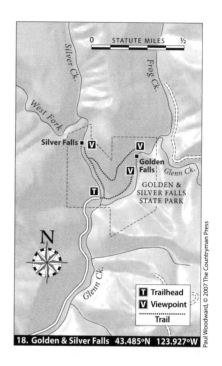

riods of high flow, Silver Creek appears to leap off the basalt protrusion at the top of the cliff. In the late summer, the falls is reduced to a small trickle.

The two viewpoints offer the best vantage for photography. However, if you are a bit adventurous and would like a different vantage point, continue up along the main trail, along the sheer cliff to the top of Golden Falls.

19

SWEET CREEK FALLS

Location: Siuslaw National Forest

Maps: USGS–Goodwin Peak

Stream: Sweet Creek

Round Trip Hike Distance:
Homestead Trail, 2.5 miles;

Sweet Creek Trail, 0.75 mile

Difficulty: Easy

Height: 75 feet

Volume: Medium

Best Season: Early spring, late fall

SPECIAL NOTES: No fees or permits are required. The Homestead Trail is an easy 1.5-mile hike that follows the creek and passes as many as nine unnamed waterfalls, ranging from 5 to 15 feet high. The trail ends at the base of Sweet Creek Falls.

DIRECTIONS: From Florence, follow OR 126 east 15 miles, to the small town of Mapleton. After crossing the Siuslaw River, make an immediate right turn onto Sweet Creek Road and follow it 10 miles to either the Homestead trailhead, or continue on another 0.75 mile to the signed Sweet Creek Falls trailhead.

THE FALLS: The valley was originally homesteaded in 1879 by the Oregon Trail pioneering family of Zarah and Cecil Sweet, and portions of the trail incorporate their old wagon road.

If you begin at the Homestead trailhead, follow the path from the parking area and head upstream. Almost immediately the trail passes a 10-foot-high double waterfall. As you continue on beneath the canopy of towering Douglas fir, alder, and maple, the trail begins to hug the canyon wall while the creek passes through in a series of small punchbowl-shaped waterfalls. Another 0.25 mile brings you to a 10-foot-high curtain tumbling over a sandstone ledge. At the 1.25-mile mark, you arrive at the plunge pool of the 20-foot-high cascade of Sweet Creek Falls. Take the short trail spur to the right to view the upper portion of the falls, where the creek is squeezed into a narrow channel before tumbling down to the second tier.

If you choose to begin at the Sweet Creek trailhead, from the parking area the trail heads down to the creek, joining the main trail 0.25 mile below Sweet Creek Falls.

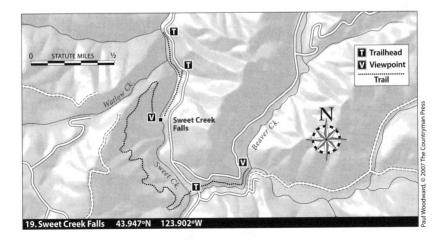

0   STATUTE MILES   ½

T Trailhead
V Viewpoint
Trail

Watlow Ck.

V Sweet Creek Falls

Beaver Ck.

N

Sweet Ck.

19. Sweet Creek Falls   43.947°N   123.902°W

Paul Woodward, © 2007 The Countryman Press

20

KENTUCKY FALLS

Location: Siuslaw National Forest

Maps: USGS–Mercer Lake, USFS: Siuslaw National Forest

Stream: Kentucky Creek, Smith River (north fork)

Round Trip Hike Distance: 4.25 miles

Difficulty: Moderate

Height: Upper Kentucky Falls, 90 feet; Lower Kentucky Falls, 100 feet; North Fork Falls, 100 feet

Volume: Medium

Best Season: Spring, summer, fall

SPECIAL NOTES: No permits or access fees are required. This moderate hike takes you into the heart of Oregon's coastal rainforest, and provides you with views of three incredible waterfalls. There are several steep drop-offs along the trail, and care should be taken when hiking with small children.

DIRECTIONS: From Eugene, follow US 126 west 33 miles to the Whitaker Creek Recreation Area sign, and turn left. From Florence, follow US 126 east 26 miles to the Whitaker Creek Recreation Area sign, and turn right. Follow the road south 1.5 miles and turn right across the bridge. Another 1.5 miles will bring you to Dunn Ridge Road. Turn left, and follow the road for 7 miles to Knowles Creek Road. Turn left onto the gravel Knowles Creek Road and follow it 2.75 miles, past the recent logging activities, to FS 23. Turn right, and follow the road 1.5 miles to FS 2300-919. Turn right again and follow the paved FS 2300-919 for 2.75 miles, to the trailhead parking area on the right.

Although the drive to the trailhead is long, winding, and an exercise in trust, it also offers some amazing views, especially along Dunn Ridge. Looking east over the countless ridges of the Oregon Coast Range and Cascade foothills are the snow-tipped Cascade peaks of The Three Sisters and Mount Bachelor.

THE FALLS: Tumbling over a 15-million-year-old basalt cliff, once part of the Pacific Ocean seafloor, are some of the most scenic waterfalls in the Coast Range. The trail's location is far enough inland to be sheltered from the millions of tourists who visit the Oregon Coast each year.

The trailhead is located on the left, just up the road from the parking area. The trail begins along Kentucky Creek, through moss-covered, old-growth Douglas fir and hemlock. Some of these ancient trees are more

Upper Kentucky Falls

than 8 feet in diameter and 300 feet high. After a 0.75-mile forest walk, the creek begins to drop away, and switchbacks, cut into the basalt cliff, carry you down to the base of the 90-foot-tall, tiered Upper Kentucky Falls.

Continuing along the trail, you gradually lose sight of Kentucky Creek, although it is always within earshot. You soon encounter a short log bridge crossing a small seasonal creek. A little more than 0.25 mile brings you to a second, larger log footbridge leading over Kentucky Creek. Another series of switchbacks will lead you 0.75 mile down to the Smith River and the observation platform for Lower Kentucky Falls.

The single-tiered, 100-foot-high falls is tucked away in a dell, surrounded by moss-covered fir and alder. Just to the left of Lower Kentucky Falls, cascading over the same basalt cliff, is the 100-foot fan of North Fork Falls on the Smith River. The flight of stairs off the observation platform joins a short path leading to a small bench, just above the confluence of Kentucky Creek and the North Fork of the Smith River. This is the best place to photograph if you wish to get both waterfalls in the same image. If you do scramble down to the water's edge, watch for the broad-leafed, and very thorny, devil's club that grows all along the creek.

The return trip is all uphill, so take some time to rest and watch the American dippers as they dart among the rocks and under the water near Upper Kentucky Falls. Also watch for Roosevelt elk, which are numerous in the area.

In addition to the fir and hemlock, early spring brings trillium, shooting stars, monkeyflower, and a few rhododendrons. A little later in the year you may be able to find a handful of salmonberries for an extra boost of energy on the way back.

21

COQUILLE RIVER FALLS

Location: Siskiyou National Forest
Maps: USGS–Illahe (see map on p. 26)
Stream: Coquille River (South Fork)
Round Trip Hike Distance: 0.5 mile

Difficulty: Easy
Height: 60 feet
Volume: Large
Best Season: Spring, summer, fall, winter

SPECIAL NOTES: No fees or permits are required. The path to the second viewpoint is not recommended for small children.

DIRECTIONS: From Roseburg, travel west on US 42 to South Fork Coquille River road, located 3 miles east of Myrtle Point. Turn south and follow it 34 miles, through Powers toward Agness. Turn left onto FS 3348, following the signs to Squaw Lake Campground. After 1.5 miles, you arrive at the marked pullout for Coquille River Falls.

THE FALLS: From the parking area, the well-maintained trail descends moderately through a series of switchbacks for 0.5 mile, before reaching the first viewpoint located just downstream from the falls. Along the way, you pass through towering Douglas fir and red cedar with an understory of salal, Oregon grape, and sword fern. The trail also passes by Drowned Out Creek, as it tumbles over moss-covered rocks in a series of 5- to 15-foot-high cascades.

The viewpoint offers great views, as the Coquille River is first split in two by the rock outcropping at the head of the falls, and then plunges 60 feet to the channeled rocks below.

The best place to photograph the falls is from the rocks just a few feet in front of the viewpoint. Be very cautious if you do choose to venture onto them, since they can be extremely slick.

II. Washington Cascades

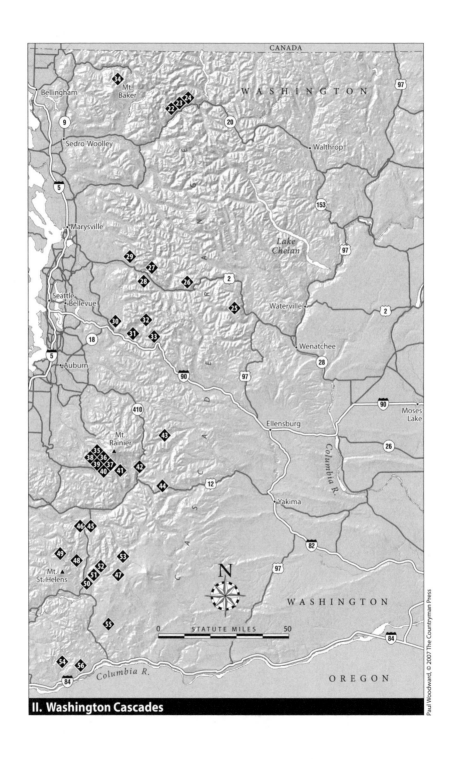

II. Washington Cascades

INTRODUCTION

The Washington Cascades run from the North Cascades National Park, on the Canadian border, south to the Columbia River. Like Oregon, they divide the state, separating the relatively low and wet western valleys from the high eastern desert, and the highly populated western cities from the more sparsely populated farmlands to the east.

Although the Washington Cascades occupy a smaller geographical area, they tend to be higher, more rugged, and more remote. The size difference is punctuated by Mount Rainier which, at 14,410 feet, stands more than 3,000 feet taller than Oregon's Mount Hood (11,235 feet). The Cascades are also home to two of Washington's three National Parks (North Cascades and Mount Rainier) and 15 National Wilderness Areas.

Like Oregon, the Washington Cascades are still very active. In 1980, Mount St. Helens erupted in an explosion that devastated nearly 150 square miles of the surrounding forest. In 2005 Mount St. Helens once again began an eruptive cycle. However, unlike the massive explosion of 1980, the most recent eruption has consisted of rebuilding the mountain. The volcano has been extruding new rock into the crater at a rate of 1 cubic yard every second!

Climate

In the higher elevations of Mount Baker and Mount Rainier, the seasonal snowfall is between 400 inches and 600 inches. Some of the greatest snowfall levels in the United States have been recorded in the Washington Cascades. In the 1998–99 snow season, Mount Baker set a new record of 1,140 inches, which broke the previous record of 1,122 inches held by Mount Rainier. However, the rest of the western Cascades receive between 50 inches and 75 inches annually. The eastern slopes receive considerably less and may see as little as 15 inches annually. Summer temperatures in the higher elevations are typically in the 60s or 70s in the day, but can easily drop below freezing at night. Temperatures in the lower elevations are roughly 5 to 10 degrees warmer.

Precautions

Many of the trails pass by steep cliffs and rushing whitewater, and in many instances the edge can be unstable and/or slippery. Stay on the trails in these areas, and refrain from climbing over fences and railings.

When hiking at high elevations, even on short trails, it is important to carry plenty of extra water along and to take your time.

Weather can change without warning, and snow is possible during any season. If your travels take you over mountain passes, make sure to check conditions before setting out.

Attractions

- North Cascades National Park is located on the border with Canada. The park is home to more than 300 glaciers nestled against jagged peaks in some of the most remote areas in the lower 48 states. The three park units—North Cascades, Ross Lake, and Lake Chelan—draw boaters, kayakers, hikers, and climbers from around the nation. Those who just want a scenic drive should take some time and travel The North Cascades Scenic Highway (US 20), which is the only developed road passing through the park. This National Scenic Byway passes through towering forests and narrow river gorges, and over spectacular mountain passes.
- The nation's fifth national park, Mount Rainier, was established in 1899. In addition to the massive 14,000-foot-high peak, the park is home to countless waterfalls and miles of hiking trails. However, perhaps the biggest draw is the unparalleled spring wildflower bloom of the Paradise Valley meadows.
- In 1980 Mount St. Helens roared back to life in a cataclysmic eruption that ejected more than a cubic mile, and the top 1,500 feet of the mountain, into the atmosphere and surrounding forest. The eruption killed 56 people and devastated more than 150 square miles of the surrounding area. Observation centers within the Mount St. Helens National Volcanic Monument tell a detailed story of the Cascade volcanoes, the 1980 eruption, and nature's own recovery efforts.

22

LADDER CREEK FALLS

Location: North Cascades National Park
Maps: USGS–Diablo Dam
Stream: Ladder Creek
Round Trip Hike Distance: 0.25 mile
Difficulty: Easy
Height: 100 feet
Volume: Medium
Best Season: Spring, summer, fall

SPECIAL NOTES: No fees or access permits are required.

DIRECTIONS: In the town of Newhalem, along US 20, park next to the Gorge Powerhouse.

THE FALLS: From the power station, follow the well-marked trail across the suspension bridge and through the gardens to a series of viewing decks overlooking the falls. Ladder Creek cascades down a narrow, moss-covered, and overhanging gorge in three tiers totaling 100 feet. The site is maintained by Seattle City Light and during the summer season, the gardens and falls are illuminated.

The falls are in the shade for the majority of the day. Photographers will want to use a warming filter and polarizing filter.

23

GORGE CREEK FALLS

Location: North Cascades National Park	roadside
	Difficulty: Easy
Maps: USGS–Gorge Dam	**Height:** 242 feet
Stream: Gorge Creek	**Volume:** Small
Round Trip Hike Distance: At	**Best Season:** Spring, summer, fall

SPECIAL NOTES: No fees or access permits are required.

DIRECTIONS: The well-marked parking area is located 3 miles east of Newhalem on US 20.

THE FALLS: From the parking area, walk across the bridge and along the pedestrian walkway to view the falls. The deck of the bridge is made from a metal grating which allows you to look through it and into the bottom of the gorge several hundred feet below. The falls itself is aptly named, as the narrow ribbon of water enters the gorge from the side and then cascades down the deep and narrow gorge in several tiers.

The bridge is the best, and only, place to photograph the falls. To minimize vibration, make sure there is no traffic crossing the bridge when the shutter is tripped. Lighting can be a problem and it is best on overcast days.

Gorge Creek Falls

24

KETCHUM CREEK FALLS

Location: North Cascades
National Park
Maps: USGS–Gorge Dam
Stream: Ketchum Creek
Round Trip Hike Distance: At

roadside
Difficulty: Easy
Height: 150 feet
Volume: Small
Best Season: Spring, summer, fall

SPECIAL NOTES: No fees or access permits are required.

DIRECTIONS: From Newhalem, follow US 20 east 4 miles to the un-marked pullout at the base of the falls.

THE FALLS: Ketchum Creek Falls begins by first plunging 50 feet over a rocky overhang, before spreading out to cascade down the re-maining 100 feet and into a jumble of large boulders.

This is a very scenic falls located right next to the road. The warm light of the early morning hours provides the best light for photographers.

25

DRURY FALLS

Location: Wenatchee National
Forest
Maps: USGS–Winton
Stream: Fall Creek
Round Trip Hike Distance: At

roadside
Difficulty: Easy
Height: Unknown
Volume: Small
Best Season: Spring, fall

SPECIAL NOTES: No fees or access permits are required.

DIRECTIONS: From Leavenworth, travel 5.5 miles west on US 2 to a small unmarked pullout.

THE FALLS: During the spring melt this waterfall is impossible to ig-nore. From the small pullout, look across the Wenatchee River to Fall Creek as it plunges over the rim of the Tumwater Canyon and disappears into a cloud of mist as it strikes the rocks below. Although not officially measured, the falls appears to be at least 500 to 600 feet high.

The waterfall faces due west so the late afternoon hours provide the best light for photography. A moderate telephoto lens will be required along with a polarizing filter and, if the air is not perfectly clear, a UV or haze filter.

26

ALPINE FALLS

Location: Mt. Baker–Snoqualmie National Forest
Maps: USGS–Scenic
Stream: Tye River
Round Trip Hike Distance: At roadside

Difficulty: Easy
Height: 40 feet
Volume: Large
Best Season: Spring, summer, fall, winter

SPECIAL NOTES: No fees or access permits are required.

DIRECTIONS: Drive east on US 2 for 8.5 miles from Skykomish to an unmarked pullout on the right just past the bridge crossing the Tye River.

THE FALLS: Several very short, informal trails lead from the parking

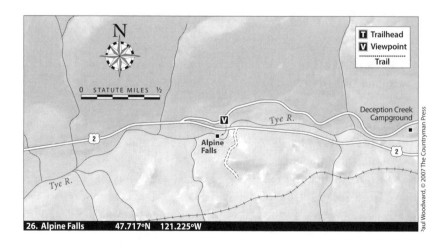

area down to the river, both above the falls and to the rocky banks of the river at its base. The Tye River passes through an undercut and moss-lined notch in the surrounding rock, just before spreading out and sliding down a 40-foot granite face and into a deep-green pool. Cedar, Douglas fir, and hemlock line the river, making this a very scenic waterfall.

Lighting can be difficult and this is a waterfall best photographed on an overcast day. As with the vast majority of waterfalls taking a slide form, a polarizing filter is recommended.

27

SUNSET FALLS

Location: Mt. Baker–Snoqualmie
National Forest
Maps: USGS–Index
Stream: Skykomish River (South
Fork)
Round Trip Hike Distance: At

roadside
Difficulty: Easy
Height: 104 feet
Volume: Large
Best Season: Spring, summer, fall,
winter

SPECIAL NOTES: No fees or access permits are required. Note: as of the writing of this book access to the falls has been limited. Check access regulations prior to visiting the falls.

DIRECTIONS: From Everett, follow US 2 for 35 miles, passing through Monroe and Sultan to Mount Index Road, just 0.25 mile past the turnoff for the small town of Index. Turn right, and follow Mount Index Road for 2 miles to the parking area.

THE FALLS: The largest waterfall along the South Fork Skykomish River, Sunset Falls drops 104 feet as it slides down a narrow granite chute and into a huge green pool at the base. The best view of the falls is from across the pool.

28

BRIDAL VEIL FALLS

Location: Mt. Baker–Snoqualmie
National Forest

Maps: USGS–Index

Stream: Bridal Veil Creek

Round Trip Hike Distance: 4

miles

Difficulty: Moderate

Height: Unknown

Volume: Medium

Best Season: Spring, summer, fall

SPECIAL NOTES: A Northwest Forest Pass is required to park at the trailhead and is available at all ranger stations, as well as many private vendors.

DIRECTIONS: From Everett, follow US 2 for 35 miles, passing through Monroe and Sultan, to Mount Index Road, just 0.25 mile past the turnoff for the small town of Index. Turn right and follow Mount Index Road for 0.5 mile to the parking area for the trailhead on the right.

THE FALLS: The waters from Lake Serene cascade down the slopes of Mount Index in a multitude of tiers and segments. This makes gauging the height of this waterfall difficult. Estimates range from between several hundred feet to more than a thousand feet. Taking a conservative approach, and including only the bottom tiers, the waterfall is approximately 500 feet high.

The waterfall is clearly visible from US 2 as you approach the town of Index. To experience the falls, start at the trailhead and follow the trail as it passes through second-growth Douglas fir and hemlock for 1.5 miles, to a trail junction. Turn right, and follow

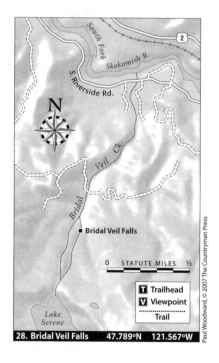

28. Bridal Veil Falls   47.789°N   121.567°W

the trail another 0.5 mile to the middle segment of the falls, which slides 200 feet down the rock face.

Continuing along the main trail for another 0.25 mile, it leads to a footbridge crossing the Bridal Veil Creek just below the lower tier. From here, you can look up at the convoluted segments of the falls as they spread out and cascade 300 feet down a jagged rock cliff.

Photographers should give up on trying to capture the entire falls in one image and concentrate on small segments of the falls. The waterfall faces west and the best light is in the late afternoon hours.

29

WALLACE FALLS

Location: Wallace Falls State Park
Maps: USGS–Gold Bar
Stream: Wallace River
Round Trip Hike Distance: 6 miles

Difficulty: Moderate
Height: 265 feet
Volume: Medium
Best Season: Spring, summer, fall, winter

SPECIAL NOTES: A Washington State Parks day-use pass is required and is available at the park entrance.

DIRECTIONS: From Monroe, follow US 2 east 12 miles to Gold Bar. From Gold Bar, follow the Wallace Falls State Park signs 2 miles to the park entrance and trailhead.

THE FALLS: With the name "Wallace," it might be assumed that the falls were named for an early pioneer. However, "Wallace" is actually derived from the last name of Joe and Sarah Kwayaylsh, members of the indigenous Skykomish tribe and early homesteaders in the area.

The trail begins by following a set of powerlines for 0.25 mile before entering the fir and hemlock forest where, after a short distance, it forks. At the fork, stay to the right, following the Woody Trail which forks again at an old railroad grade. Veer to the left and follow the trail as it gradually climbs, while paralleling the alder-lined Wallace River. Stay to the right at the next two junctions, at the 1.5 and 2.5 mile marks, separated by the bridge crossing the North Fork of the Wallace River. A short 0.25 mile after the second junction, the trail arrives at the first viewpoint of the two-tiered, 265-foot-high, falls.

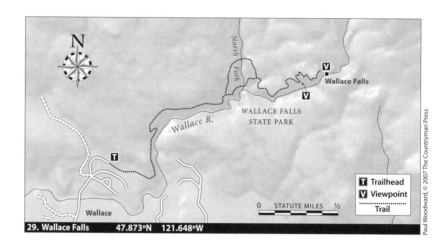

29. Wallace Falls   47.873°N   121.648°W

Paul Woodward, © 2007 The Countryman Press

The Wallace River plunges over a basalt cliff and into a deep circular pool that is surrounded by a dense forest of fir, hemlock, and cedar. The river then pours out of the pool and cascades through a narrow gorge forming the second tier.

Continue up along the trail, for another half mile, to reach the upper viewpoint overlooking the top tier and surrounding valley.

30

SNOQUALMIE FALLS

Location: Snoqualmie

Maps: USGS–Snoqualmie

Stream: Snoqualmie River

Round Trip Hike Distance:
1 mile

Difficulty: Moderate

Height: 268 feet

Volume: Large

Best Season: Spring, summer, fall, winter

SPECIAL NOTES: This is one of Washington State's most popular natural attractions, receiving more than 1 million visitors each year, so be prepared for crowds. The parking area next to the gift shop has a one-hour limit, so if you intend to hike to the base of the falls, park in the area across the road from the Snoqualmie Falls Lodge. No fees or permits are required.

Snoqualmie Falls

DIRECTIONS: From the town of Snoqualmie, travel west following the Snoqualmie Falls signs on SR 202 for 2 miles to the parking area. If you are coming from Fall City you will cross the Snoqualmie River and travel east on SR 202, again following the Snoqualmie Falls signs, 3.5 miles to the parking area.

THE FALLS: From the parking area, it's just a short stroll to the viewpoint along the gorge rim. While a slightly elevated and covered viewing platform offers the best view of the falls, views are abundant all along the paved rim path. From here, you can watch the Snoqualmie River glide past the Snoqualmie Falls Lodge and plummet 268 feet to the large plunge pool below. During periods of low flow the falls is split in two by a rock outcropping at the top of the falls, but during periods of high flow it forms a tremendous broad curtain. Even thought the falls is a good 0.12 mile away you can still feel the spray as it curls up above the gorge rim.

In the early 1900s, Puget Power built a small hydroelectric facility beneath the falls and the outlet can be seen on the far side, near the base of the falls. The facility is still in operation and provides power to more than 16,000 local residents.

While the rim offers a beautiful overall view of the falls and lodge precariously perched above the waterfall, the trail to the base offers an opportunity to experience the true power of the falls. The steep 0.5 mile path leads you to the plunge pool directly beneath the rim viewpoint. If you do make the hike, plan on getting wet, and if you are photographing make sure to bring some protection for your camera and equipment.

31

TWIN FALLS

Location: Snoqualmie National Forest

Maps: USGS–Snoqualmie Pass

Stream: Snoqualmie River (South Fork)

Round Trip Hike Distance: 2.75 miles

Difficulty: Moderate

Height: Twin Falls, 135 feet; Middle Twin Falls, 25 feet; Upper Twin Falls, 35 feet

Volume: Medium

Best Season: Spring, summer, fall

SPECIAL NOTES: A Washington State Parks day-use pass is required and is available at the trailhead.

DIRECTIONS: From Snoqualmie, follow I-90 east 11 miles to Exit 34. Turn right at the bottom of the exit ramp onto Edgewick Road, and follow it 0.75 mile to S.E. 159th. Turn left onto 159th, and follow it another 0.5 mile to the trailhead.

THE FALLS: The trail heads upstream from the parking area, along the river and under a canopy of fir, cedar, and alder. After a little more than a 0.25 mile, the trail leaves the river and begins a gradual climb through the forest and over a small ridge. From the ridgetop, the trail

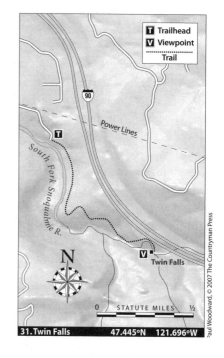

Twin Falls

offers a nice view of the river below. From here, the trail begins a moderate descent back down to the river and a huge old-growth Douglas fir that has been fenced off. Although the old tree has since succumbed to the elements, it is still an impressive sight.

From the tree, the trail once again begins to climb until it soon reaches an unmarked trail spur to the right. Follow the spur, which after a few hundred feet leads to a wooden observation platform perched precariously on the cliff overlooking the falls. The platform offers a great view, as the South Fork of the Snoqualmie River half-slides and half-veils gracefully, over a convoluted rock face, into a deep blue-green pool.

Back on the main trail, continue upstream another few hundred yards to the 25-foot-high Middle Twin Falls. Here the river winds its way through a narrow rock channel, creating a double punchbowl as it passes by moss-covered rocks.

Another few hundred yards, and the trail arrives at the third and final waterfall in the Twin Falls series. Under a canopy of cedar, the river cascades 35 feet down another narrow, moss-lined channel and into a deep pool.

Photographers will have difficulties with the light on sunny days, and this series of waterfalls is best shot on a more overcast day. A wide-angle lens, polarizing filter, and a warming filter will all be put to good use here.

32

OTTER FALLS AND MARTEN CREEK FALLS

Location: Snoqualmie National Forest

Maps: USGS–Snoqualmie Lake

Stream: Otter Creek; Marten Creek

Round Trip Hike Distance: Marten Creek Falls, 4.5 miles;

Otter Falls, 7.5 miles

Difficulty: Moderate

Height: Otter Falls, 700 feet; Marten Creek Falls, 50 feet

Volume: Small

Best Season: Spring, fall

SPECIAL NOTES: A Northwest Forest Pass is required in order to park at the trailhead, and is available at all ranger stations as well as from many private vendors.

DIRECTIONS: From North Bend, follow I-90 east 2 miles to Edgewick Road (Exit 34). Turn left, follow 468th Avenue 0.5 mile to Taylor River Road, and turn right. Follow Taylor River Road for 11.5 miles to its end and the trailhead for the Taylor River Trail.

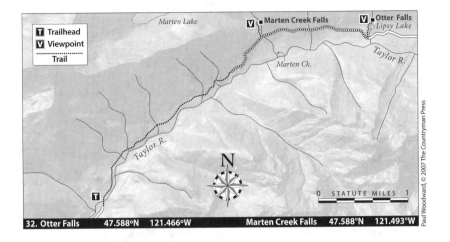

32. Otter Falls 47.588°N 121.466°W | **Marten Creek Falls** 47.588°N 121.493°W

THE FALLS: The trail begins by crossing the Taylor River, and then sets off through a second-growth forest of fir, hemlock, and alder as it follows an old logging road. After 0.25 mile, the trail forks. Follow the trail to the right, as it parallels the Taylor River. This mostly level trail continues along the river for another 2 miles, where it crosses Marten Creek just below Marten Creek Falls. A faint trail leads upstream a few hundred feet, and provides a better view of the 50-foot-high falls as it thunders through a narrow slot in the rock and into a tumultuous, deep-green pool.

Continue along the main trail for another 0.5 mile, where it arrives at the first of two small, shallow creeks to be forded. The second ford is encountered another 0.5 mile down the trail. The trail arrives at Otter Creek 0.5 mile after the second fording. After crossing Otter Creek, an unmarked trail to the left leads up steeply for a few hundred yards, and then down to the shore of Lipsy Lake at the base of Otter Falls. The falls is 700 feet high. The first half of the waterfall is a cascade, which then spreads out and slides down the smooth, granite rock face and into Lipsy Lake.

Marten Creek Falls faces southeast, while Otter Falls faces due south, so the best light for photographers is in the morning. A wide-angle lens and polarizing filter will be useful.

33

FRANKLIN FALLS

Location: Snoqualmie National
Forest
Maps: USGS–Snoqualmie Pass
Stream: Snoqualmie River (South
Fork)
Round Trip Hike Distance: 2

miles
Difficulty: Easy
Height: 70 feet
Volume: Medium
Best Season: Spring, summer, fall

SPECIAL NOTES: No fees or access permits are required.

DIRECTIONS: From Snoqualmie, follow I-90 east 24 miles to Exit 47. Turn left at the bottom of the exit ramp, and then right at the next junction onto FS 58. Follow FS 58 for 3.25 miles, passing Denny Creek Campground, and then turn left, following the signs for Franklin Falls.

THE FALLS: From the parking area next to the bridge, the trail begins its climb upstream along Denny Creek. A few old-growth fir and cedar line the trail as it climbs moderately above the creek. Just before the trail descends to Franklin Falls, it encounters a signed junction. To reach the falls continue straight on the main trail as it descends, steeply at times, to the base of the waterfall.

The falls plunge 70 feet, down a colorful rock face and into a clear pool lined by a pebbly beach. During the hot summer months the falls can be a popular destination for families looking to cool down by wading in the pool, or just soaking in the spray from the falls.

Photographers will want to

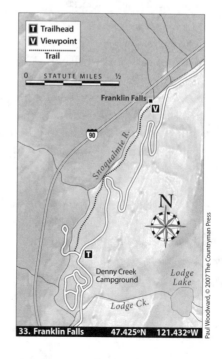

Trailhead
Viewpoint
Trail

0 STATUTE MILES ½

Franklin Falls

90

Snoqualmie R.

N

Denny Creek
Campground

Lodge
Lake

Lodge Ck.

33. Franklin Falls   47.425°N   121.432°W

Paul Woodward, © 2007 The Countryman Press

arrive early, not only for the best light, but to also avoid the summer crowds. A polarizing filter will help bring out the color in the cliff.

34

NOOKSACK FALLS AND WELLS CREEK FALLS

Location: Snoqualmie National Forest

Maps: USGS–Bearpaw Mountain, Mount Baker

Stream: Nooksack River (North Fork); Wells Creek

Round Trip Hike Distance: At roadside

Difficulty: Easy

Height: Nooksack Falls, 88 feet; Wells Creek Falls, 110 feet

Volume: Large

Best Season: Spring, summer, fall, winter

SPECIAL NOTES: No fees or access permits are required.

DIRECTIONS: From the small town of Maple Falls, follow US 542 east 14.5 miles to Wells Creek Road and turn right, following the signs for Nooksack Falls. Follow the road 0.75 mile to the parking area for Nooksack Falls, on the left.

To visit Wells Creek Falls, continue another 5.25 miles past the parking area for Nooksack Falls on Wells Creek Road, to the bridge crossing Wells Creek.

THE FALLS: A very short path leads to a railed viewpoint overlooking this popular roadside attraction. The waters of the North Fork of the Nooksack River, which originates on the flanks of nearby Mount Shuksan, are funneled down the rocky canyon, where it then collects into a beautiful blue-green pool, just before it plunges into the narrow gorge below the falls. A short rock pinnacle at the head of the falls splits the river into two segments just as it plunges over the rim, with the majority of the river following the left segment.

Wells Creek Falls is located just a short distance past the parking area for Nooksack Falls, and is visible from Wells Creek Road. However, to get an even better view follow the creek upstream a few hundred yards into the canyon. The falls is situated at the head of the narrow, moss-lined rock amphitheater, where Wells Creek pours through a notch that it has cut into the rim of the basalt cliff, plunging 110 feet into a small blue pool.

To avoid issues with contrast, photographers will want to arrive at both falls in the late afternoon hours, after the sunlight is off the water. Both of these falls also kick up a large amount of spray, so extra protection for camera gear is recommended.

35

CHRISTINE FALLS

Location: Mount Rainier National Park

Maps: USGS–Mt. Rainier West

Stream: Van Trump Creek

Round Trip Hike Distance: At roadside

Difficulty: Easy

Height: 75 feet

Volume: Medium

Best Season: Spring, summer, fall, winter

SPECIAL NOTES: A National Park entrance fee is required at the entrance station.

DIRECTIONS: Christine Falls is located along the park road (SR 706) 2.5 miles east of the Cougar Rock Campground. A well-marked, and often crowded, parking area is located on the east side of the bridge crossing Van Trump Creek.

THE FALLS: Van Trump Creek is named for Philemon Beecher Van Trump, who was one of the two men to first summit Mount Rainier in 1870; the other was Hazard Stevens. The waterfall is named for Van Trump's daughter.

From the parking area, a short set of stairs leads downstream to a fenced overlook of the lower tier as it passes under the signature arched stone bridge, which was built in the 1930s. This is the most popular view of the falls, and the one to be most likely seen on the postcards sold in gift shops within the park.

To view the upper tier of the falls, follow the path back to the parking area and walk along the bridge. Van Trump Creek cascades through a narrow gorge and beneath the bridge.

Christine Falls

This is perhaps the most photographed falls in the park, and access to it is very limited, so trying to gain a unique perspective is next to impossible. Sunrise and sunset provide the best light for photography.

36

CARTER FALLS AND MADCAP FALLS

Location: Mount Rainier National Park

Maps: USGS–Mount Rainer West

Stream: Paradise River

Round Trip Hike Distance: 2.75 miles

Difficulty: Easy

Height: Carter Falls, 60 feet; Madcap Falls, 25 Feet

Volume: Medium

Best Season: Spring, summer, fall

SPECIAL NOTES: A National Park entrance fee is required at the entrance station.

DIRECTIONS: The Cougar Rock Campground is located 8 miles east of the Nisqually entrance station on the main park road (SR 706). The marked trailhead is located on the left, across from the entrance to the campground.

THE FALLS: The trail, which is just one short section of the 93-mile-long Wonderland Trail that circumnavigates the mountain, begins by crossing the Nisqually River on a log bridge. The trail then continues along the river, following an old wooden water pipe, as it climbs above the alder and into the old-growth Douglas fir and hemlock. After 0.25 mile, the trail joins the Paradise River, and follows it another 1 mile to the 60-foot-high Carter Falls, as the Paradise River plunges through a small notch in the cliff and into a frothing shallow pool below.

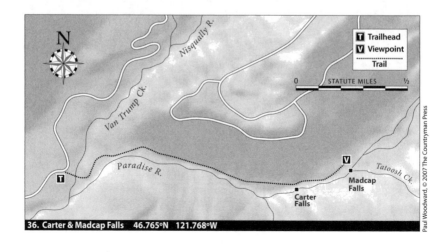

36. Carter & Madcap Falls   46.765°N   121.768°W

Paul Woodward, © 2007 The Countryman Press

To reach Madcap Falls, continue along the trail for another few hundred yards. Here, the Paradise River slides over a 25-foot-high series of mossy rock shelves, underneath a canopy of fir and cedar. In the spring, the wildflowers that Mount Rainier is known for line the banks of the river.

The best light for photographing both of the waterfalls is in the late afternoon hours.

37

COMET FALLS

Location: Mount Rainier National Park
Maps: USGS–Mount Rainer West
Stream: Van Trump Creek
Round Trip Hike Distance: 3.25 miles
Difficulty: Moderate
Height: 320 feet
Volume: Medium
Best Season: Spring, summer, fall

SPECIAL NOTES: A National Park entrance fee is required at the entrance station. This is one of the park's more popular trails, and the parking area can fill quickly during the summer months.

DIRECTIONS: The trailhead is located along the park road (SR 706) 2.25 miles east of the Cougar Rock Campground. A designated parking area is located on the left side of the road.

THE FALLS: From the parking area, the trail climbs steeply through the old-growth forest and crosses above Christine Falls after 0.25 mile, then parallels Van Trump Creek. Along the way, the trail crosses several open avalanche chutes that have been carved out of the forest. During the winter months the chutes can be deadly, but during the spring and summer they provide open alleys of sunlight for wildflowers to thrive.

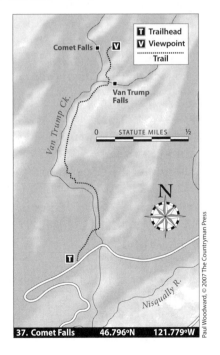

One mile past Christine Falls, the trail crosses the East Fork of Van Trump Creek just below the 120-foot-high, three-tiered Van Trump Falls as it slides and plunges down a narrow chute. After crossing the bridge the trail yields its first glimpses of Comet Falls as it climbs up through a short series of switchbacks. After a quarter mile, the trail reaches the base of the two-tiered, 320-foot-high falls as it plummets off a towering basalt cliff and into a barren rocky amphitheater. The first tier is a lacey 300 feet high, and is followed by a 20-foot-high second tier.

A short trail spur used to lead to a beautiful plunge pool at the falls' base. However, a debris flow in 2001 has since filled it with rocks and silt, so this side trail is no longer easily negotiable.

The falls is in full sun until midday, so photographers will either want to arrive at sunrise or the late afternoon hours. A polarizing filter, warming filter, and graduated neutral density filter are recommended equipment.

38

NARADA FALLS

Location: Mount Rainier National Park

Maps: USGS–Mount Rainer East

Stream: Paradise River

Round Trip Hike Distance: 2.75 miles

Difficulty: Easy

Height: 168 feet

Volume: Medium

Best Season: Spring, summer, fall

SPECIAL NOTES: A National Park entrance fee is required at the entrance station. The upper viewpoint overlooking the falls is wheelchair accessible.

DIRECTIONS: Narada Falls is located along the park road (SR 706) 6 miles east of the Cougar Rock Campground. A large, well-marked, and crowded parking area is located on the right side of the road.

THE FALLS: The viewpoint near the parking area is located on the brink of the falls, and overlooks the Paradise River as it disappears over the cliff. To get a much better view of the falls, follow the trail as it crosses the river and winds steeply down 0.25 mile, to several viewpoints approximately halfway down the opposite side of the cliff. From here, mist from the falls rolls up and perpetually bathes the trail as the river cascades 168 feet down a rock face of columnar basalt in a broad veil. In the afternoon hours, as the sun illuminates the falls, it frequently produces a rainbow at its base. Narada is the Hindu word for "pure" and when the rainbow makes its appearance, it easy to see how the waterfall was named.

In order to capture the rainbow, photographers will want to arrive in the mid- to late-afternoon hours, when the entire waterfall is still illuminated by the sun. Use a polarizing filter to help bring out the color in the rainbow. Spray from the falls is also a concern, and photographers will want to take appropriate measures to protect their equipment.

39

MYRTLE FALLS

Location: Mount Rainier National Park

Maps: USGS–Mount Rainer East

Stream: Edith Creek

Round Trip Hike Distance: 2.75 miles

Difficulty: Easy

Height: 60 feet

Volume: Small

Best Season: Spring, summer, fall

SPECIAL NOTES: A National Park entrance fee is required at the entrance station. Although the paths through Paradise Valley can be steep, in places the falls is wheelchair accessible.

DIRECTIONS: Myrtle Falls is located along the trails of the Paradise Valley. From the Nisqually entrance, follow the park road (SR 706) 18 miles east, to the Henry M. Jackson Memorial Visitor Center.

THE FALLS: Located along the skyline trail, Myrtle Falls is in the heart of the wildflower meadows of the Paradise Valley, making this an exceptionally scenic and photogenic waterfall during the height of the wildflower bloom in August. From the Jackson Visitor Center, follow the paved path along the Avalanche Lily Trail 0.25 mile to the intersection with the Skyline Trail just above the Paradise Inn. From the intersection, follow the Skyline Trial to the left for another 0.5 mile to the falls. In the summer the meadows are alive with color. Avalanche lilies, glacier lilies, lupine, monkeyflower, and paintbrush are just a few of the wildflowers to be encountered along the trail.

The waterfall is a 60-foot-high, segmented fan that cascades down a loose rock face and into a narrow gorge. The best view of the falls is from a short trail spur to the right, leading to a railed viewing area. From here, majestic Mount Rainier towers in the background above the wildflower meadows, the trail bridge, and Myrtle Falls.

Myrtle Falls

This is one of the premier photographic destinations in the Northwest. Photographers will want to bring everything, and they will want to arrive early, while the dew is still on the flowers and the thousands of visitors have yet to awake.

40

RUBY FALLS

Location: Mount Rainier National Park

Maps: USGS–Mount Rainer East

Stream: Paradise River

Round Trip Hike Distance: At roadside

Difficulty: Easy

Height: 30 feet

Volume: Medium

Best Season: Spring, summer, fall

SPECIAL NOTES: A National Park entrance fee is required at the entrance station.

DIRECTIONS: Ruby Falls is located just past the intersection with the one-way road leading up to the Paradise Valley. From the Nisqually entrance, follow park road (SR 706) 16 miles east to the intersection and turn right. Park at the small unmarked pullout next to the bridge crossing the Paradise River.

THE FALLS: The upper tier of the falls can be viewed from the bridge as it slides 15 feet over a series of ledges, beneath mountain hemlock. To view the second tier, cross the road and follow the Narada Falls Trail downstream a few yards where the Paradise River tumbles another 15 feet down a rock staircase into a deep-green pool.

41

MARTHA FALLS

Location: Mount Rainier National Park

Maps: USGS–Mount Rainer East

Stream: Unicorn Creek

Round Trip Hike Distance: At roadside

Difficulty: Easy

Height: 150 feet

Volume: Medium

Best Season: Spring, summer, fall

SPECIAL NOTES: A National Park entrance fee is required at the entrance station.

DIRECTIONS: From the Nisqually entrance, follow the park road (SR 706) 21.5 miles east to a broad unmarked pullout on the right, 0.25 mile before the first tunnel along Stevens Canyon. The pullout is located 13.5 miles east of the Stevens Canyon entrance station.

THE FALLS: It is very difficult to miss this waterfall as you drive along Stevens Canyon. Located on the opposite side of the canyon, Unicorn Creek first fans out as it slides 30 or 40 feet down the rim of the canyon, before plunging the final 120 feet to the rock below. The falls can also be reached via the Wonderland Trail, where it intersects with the park road. Located 0.75 miles east from the parking area for The Bench Trail, follow the trail east as it descends into the canyon. After 0.5 mile, the trail crosses Unicorn Creek, providing a view overlooking the falls.

42

OHANAPECOSH FALLS AND SILVER FALLS

Location: Mount Rainier National Park

Maps: USGS–Chinook Pass

Stream: Ohanapecosh River

Round Trip Hike Distance: Ohanapecosh Falls, 7 miles; Silver Falls, 1 mile

Difficulty: Easy to moderate

Height: Ohanapecosh Falls, 50 feet; Silver Falls, 40 feet

Volume: Medium

Best Season: Spring, summer, fall

SPECIAL NOTES: A National Park entrance fee is required at the entrance station.

DIRECTIONS: From the Stevens Canyon entrance, follow SR 706 just 0.25 mile to the parking area for the Grove of the Patriarchs Trail.

THE FALLS: The vast majority of visitors to Mount Rainier National Park merely pass through this area of the park on their way to the Paradise Valley. That leaves Ohanapecosh the perfect area to avoid the crowds. To visit Ohanapecosh Falls, follow the trail upstream through the Grove of the Patriarchs. Many of the trees in this stand of Douglas fir and cedar are over one thousand years old. With diameters of 25 to 35 feet, they tower more than 200 feet into the air.

The relatively level trail continues following the Ohanapecosh River through immense fir and cedar, with an understory of vine maple and Oregon-grape. After 0.75 mile, the trail crosses Olallie Creek, and then meanders along the river for another 2.25 miles, passing several deep-blue pools, to the bridge overlooking Ohanapecosh Falls. This two-tiered falls first drops 20 feet into a deep rock pool, which then spills down another 30 feet into a second larger pool. A short spur trail leads to a viewpoint near the base of the falls.

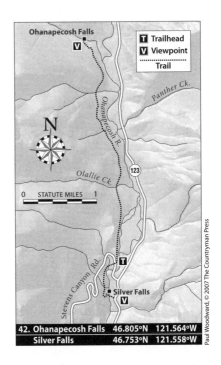

To visit Silver Falls, follow the trail downstream from the parking area for a half mile, and turn right at the trail junction. The trail leads a few hundred feet to a bridge crossing the deep gorge, just below the falls. The Ohanapecosh River thunders 40 feet down through the narrow gorge and into the deep blue pool below.

The light is best when it is not directly on the falls, so photographers will want to visit in the early morning or late afternoon hours. A warming filter will be useful for both of these falls.

43

UNION CREEK FALLS

Location: Norse Peak Wilderness Area

Maps: USGS–Goose Prairie

Stream: Union Creek

Round Trip Hike Distance: 0.5 mile

Difficulty: Easy

Height: 60 feet

Volume: Medium

Best Season: Spring, summer, fall

SPECIAL NOTES: A Northwest Forest Pass is required to park at the trailhead, and is available at ranger stations and many private vendors.

DIRECTIONS: From Chinook Pass, follow SR 410 for 7.5 miles east to the well-marked Union Creek trailhead.

THE FALLS: From the parking area, follow the trail across the creek on a small footbridge, where it makes a short climb. After 0.25 mile, the falls come into view. After a couple of switchbacks, a trail spur to the left leads down to the base of the falls. Here the waterfall fans out, as it delicately tumbles down the moss-covered basalt cliff.

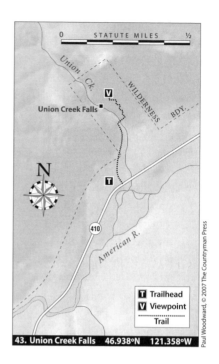

43. Union Creek Falls   46.938°N   121.358°W

Paul Woodward, © 2007 The Countryman Press

Photographers should avoid the midday sun by shooting in the morning or late afternoon hours. A warming filter and polarizing filter are recommended, as is rain protection since the falls can kick up a lot of spray.

44

CLEAR CREEK FALLS AND UPPER CLEAR CREEK FALLS

Location: Snoqualmie National Forest

Maps: USGS–Spiral Butte

Stream: Clear Creek

Round Trip Hike Distance: At roadside

Difficulty: Easy

Height: Clear Creek Falls, 300 feet; Upper Clear Creek Falls, 75 feet

Volume: Medium

Best Season: Spring, summer, fall

SPECIAL NOTES: No fees or access permits are required.

DIRECTIONS: From the White Pass Ski Area, follow US 12 east 2.5 miles to the signed pullout for Clear Creek Falls.

THE FALLS: To view Clear Creek Falls, walk downstream a few hundred feet to the fenced viewpoints looking down on this surprising 300-foot-high falls. Clear Creek first rolls over the rim of the canyon, then veils out down the canyon wall before splashing onto the rocks and into a small pool below.

To view Upper Clear Creek Falls, a waterfall with a completely different personality, walk a few hundred feet upstream from the parking area, to another set of fenced viewpoints overlooking Upper Clear Creek Falls. Here the main stream of the creek plunges down one side, while the remainder of the creek spreads out and fans down the smooth rock face and into a small green pool.

The best light for both waterfalls is early in the morning, before the sunlight has a chance to strike the falls. A polarizing filter is very helpful for the upper falls.

45

ANGEL FALLS AND COVELL CREEK FALLS

Location: Gifford Pinchot National Forest

Maps: USGS–Tower Rock

Stream: Covell Creek (West Fork), Covell Creek

Round Trip Hike Distance: 2.75 miles

Difficulty: Moderate

Height: Angel Falls, 150 feet; Covell Creek Falls, 75 feet

Volume: Small

Best Season: Spring, fall, winter

SPECIAL NOTES: A Northwest Forest Pass is required to park at the trailhead and is available at all ranger stations as well as many private vendors.

DIRECTIONS: Follow SR 131 from Randle for 23 miles and then turn right onto FS 23. Follow the signs for the Cispus Learning Center for 8 miles to FS 28. Turn right, and follow FS 28 for 2 miles to the well-marked Burley Mountain trailhead parking area on the left.

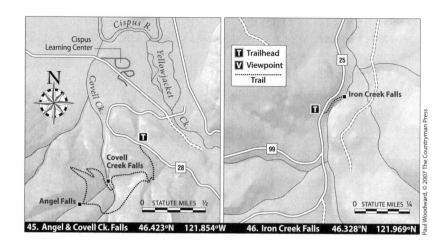

45. Angel & Covell Ck. Falls   46.423°N   121.854°W   46. Iron Creek Falls   46.328°N   121.969°N

THE FALLS: The trailhead is located across the road from the parking area. It begins with a moderately steep climb as it passes through an old-growth forest of Douglas fir and hemlock, with some alder mixed in for color in the fall. After 0.5 mile, the trail reaches a junction with the Angel Falls Loop. Stay to the left as the trail levels off and then descends to the West Fork of Covell Creek after 0.25 mile. The trail then loops below the 150-foot-high Angel Falls, as it tumbles down a basalt rock face covered with a thick layer of moss and splashes onto a bed of boulders.

To reach Covell Creek Falls, continue along the trail as it climbs another 0.25 mile to the junction with the Burley Mountain Trail. Turn right, following the Angel Falls Loop. The trail once again descends, steeply at times, through the forest with clover-like oxalis and fern lining the trail. After 0.5 mile, the trail reaches the base of the 75-foot-high Covell Creek Falls, as it plunges over an undercut basalt cliff and onto a jumble of moss- and fern-covered rocks below. Continue along the trail as it passes behind the falls, offering a very distinct perspective even when the creek flow is low.

To return back to the trailhead, continue along the trail turning right at the next junction and then left at the second junction located another 0.5 mile further down the trail. This part of the trail should look familiar, as it descends the final 0.5 mile to the parking area.

Along the trail you will notice many small caves along the cliff walls. These are actually lava tubes, remnants of the ancient basalt lava flows that created the cliffs, which the waterfalls now tumble over.

Photographers will find the best light in the late afternoon and evening hours, and they should plan to bring a wide-angle lens, polarizing filter, and graduated neutral density filter.

46

IRON CREEK FALLS

Location: Gifford Pinchot National Forest

Maps: USGS–French Butte

Stream: Iron Creek

Round Trip Hike Distance: 0.25 mile

Difficulty: Easy

Height: 30 feet

Volume: Medium

Best Season: Spring, summer, fall, winter

SPECIAL NOTES: No fees or access permits are required.

DIRECTIONS: From Randle, travel south on FS 25 for 19 miles to the well-marked parking area on the left.

THE FALLS: From the parking area, follow the well-maintained path and stone steps several hundred yards to the base of the 30-foot punchbowl. Iron Creek has carved out a narrow notch through the overhanging basalt bluff, just before it plunges into a large opalescent pool at its base. Although small in stature, the falls is quite photogenic.

47

LANGFIELD FALLS

Location: Gifford Pinchot National Forest

Maps: USGS–Sleeping Beauty

Stream: Mosquito Creek

Round Trip Hike Distance: 0.5

mile

Difficulty: Easy

Height: 70 feet

Volume: Small

Best Season: Spring, summer, fall

SPECIAL NOTES: No fees or access permits are required.

DIRECTIONS: From Trout Lake, follow SR 141 north 1.75 miles to FS 88. Turn right onto FS 88, and follow it 13 miles to Big Tire Junction. Turn right, and follow the sign to Langfield Falls.

THE FALLS: From the parking area, the wide, fir needle covered trail, descends downstream through forested dell. After a few hundred feet the

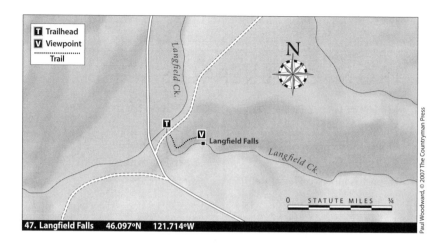

47. Langfield Falls   46.097°N   121.714°W

falls begin to come into view. The trail continues along the rim of the gorge and then arrives at a viewpoint overlooking the 70-foot-high falls. The appropriately named Mosquito Creek fans over a smooth basalt rock face and into a shallow pool. From the viewpoint, the trail continues a short distance to the edge of the pool at the base of the falls.

The falls is named for K. C. Langfield, who served as a forest service ranger from 1933 until 1956.

48

LAVA CANYON

Location: Mount St. Helens
National Volcanic Monument
Maps: USGS–Smith Creek Butte
Stream: Muddy River
Round Trip Hike Distance: 3.5
miles
Difficulty: Moderate
Height: 35–135 feet
Volume: Large
Best Season: Spring, summer, fall

SPECIAL NOTES: A Northwest Forest Pass is required to park at the trailhead, and is available at all ranger stations as well as many private vendors. The first 0.5 mile of the trail is wheelchair accessible. Due to the steep cliffs and extremely hazardous off-trail conditions, the lower portion of the trail is not recommended for small children.

DIRECTIONS: From Woodland, drive east on SR 503 for 35 miles to FS 83. Turn left, following the Lava Canyon/Ape Cave signs, and follow FS 83 another 11 miles to the road's end at the trailhead.

THE FALLS: While the north side of the mountain rightfully drew all of the attention during the 1980 eruption of Mount St. Helens, the south side did not escape completely unscathed. During the eruption, the extreme heat melted the shoestring glacier, sending its water (mixed with ash and mud), down the south side of the mountain. The concrete-like slurry rumbled down Muddy Creek, scouring the canyon bare and revealing an earlier 3,500-year-old basalt lava flow.

This trail passes several named and unnamed falls, ranging from between 35 feet to 135 feet in height. The trail sets off from a grove of Douglas fir that was spared by the 1980 lahar, but soon enters the barren canyon. Turn right at the first junction and follow it over the bridge crossing Muddy Creek, just above Upper Lava Canyon Falls. From the bridge, the creek follows a smooth rock channel carved into the ancient lava just before it plunges 75 feet into the pool below. For a better view of the falls, continue downstream along the trail to several unprotected viewpoints overlooking the falls.

Continuing along, the trail soon reaches a 200-foot-high suspension bridge re-crossing the creek. Looking upstream from mid-span on the bridge are views of several small cascades as the creek plunges from one pool to the next. Once across the bridge, turn right, and follow the trail 0.12 mile to a cliff-side view of a 25-foot-high unnamed double punchbowl.

Hikers who are nervous of heights should turn left, and follow the trail back to the trailhead. From here the trail narrows, and after another 0.12 mile passes along a 200-foot-high unprotected cliff, overlooking the 135-foot double

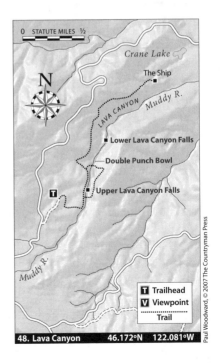

Crane Lake

The Ship

LAVA CANYON Muddy R.

Lower Lava Canyon Falls

Double Punch Bowl

Upper Lava Canyon Falls

Muddy R.

0 STATUTE MILES ½

N

Muddy R.

T Trailhead
V Viewpoint
Trail

48. Lava Canyon   46.172°N   122.081°W

Paul Woodward, © 2007 The Countryman Press

plunge of Lava Canyon Falls. This is the largest of the falls along the trail. The first tier drops 100 feet into a small rock pool, where it then spills over and cascades down another 35 feet. For another view of the falls, continue downstream where the trail uses a 40-foot steel ladder to descend a small rock bluff. From the base of the ladder, the trail soon reaches another junction. Turn right, and follow it a short 0.25 mile as it climbs a basalt tower named "The Ship." From the viewpoint atop The Ship, look back up the canyon to Lava Canyon Falls, as well as yet another 40-foot-high unnamed falls several hundred yards below Lava Canyon Falls.

49

LOOWIT FALLS

Location: Mount St. Helens
National Volcanic Monument
Maps: USGS–Mount St. Helens
Stream: Loowit Creek
Round Trip Hike Distance: 8.75

miles
Difficulty: Difficult
Height: 200 feet
Volume: Small
Best Season: Spring, summer, fall

SPECIAL NOTES: A Northwest Forest Pass is required to park at the trailhead, and is available at all ranger stations as well as from many private vendors.

DIRECTIONS: From Woodland to the trailhead at Windy Ridge it is 88 miles. Drive east on SR 503 to the town of Cougar, where SR 503 becomes SR 90. From Cougar, follow SR 90 for 6.5 miles to the Pine Creek Ranger Station. Continue straight on FS 25 (SR 90 veers right, toward Trout Lake). Follow FS 25 for another 25 miles to FS 99. Turn left onto FS 99 and follow the signs for 16 miles to the road's end at Windy Ridge.

THE FALLS: From the viewpoint at Windy Ridge, the trail to Loowit Falls is clearly visible as it passes through the barren landscape. For the first 2 miles, the trail descends along an old gravel logging road. At the road's end, the Windy Trail begins and follows a series of rock cairns across the pumice plain for 1 mile to a junction with the Loowit Trail. Turn right, and follow the trail another 1.25 miles to another junction. Turn left, and follow this short trail spur 0.25 mile, to a viewpoint looking up at

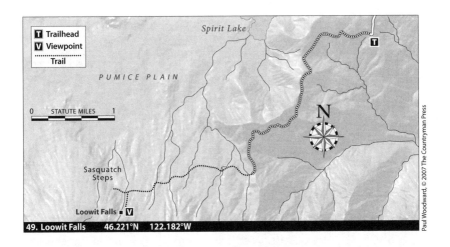

49. Loowit Falls   46.221°N   122.182°W

the 200-foot-high falls. Devoid of any vegetation, and resembling an alien landscape, Loowit Creek tumbles over a yellow-and orange-tinted ash bluff at the head of the heavily eroded canyon.

This is an eerie place, especially when you realize that only a short distance away the lava dome inside the crater is actively erupting, pushing up more than a dump truck load of new rock to the surface each minute!

On the way back, take some time to notice that the land is bouncing back. Over the pumice plains, fireweed, aster, and penstemon are all beginning to bring some color back to this previously barren landscape.

50

CURLY CREEK FALLS

Location: Gifford Pinchot National Forest

Maps: USGS–Burnt Creek

Stream: Curly Creek

Round Trip Hike Distance: 0.25 mile

Difficulty: Easy

Height: 75 feet

Volume: Medium

Best Season: Early spring, late fall

SPECIAL NOTES: The viewing area is wheelchair accessible in good weather. Early spring is the best time to view the falls; summer foliage

Curly Creek Falls

may obscure the view. A Northwest Forest Pass is required and is available at many private vendors.

DIRECTIONS: From Woodland, travel on SR 503 east, following the signs to Mount St Helens and Cougar. As you pass through the small town of Cougar, SR 503 turns into County Road 90. After you have traveled 38.5 miles from Woodland, follow the signs to Carson, as County Road 90 veers to the right just past the Pine Creek ranger station. Continue on County Road 90 for another 5.5 miles to County Road 9039 and turn left. Follow the road for 0.75 mile to the parking area on the left side of the road.

THE FALLS: From the parking area, a broad path leads down to the edge of the Lewis River canyon where it joins the Lewis River Trail. Turn right, and follow the path as it meanders along the canyon rim and through towering Douglas fir. After a few hundred yards you come to the railed viewpoint of Curly Creek Falls, located on the opposite side of the canyon. Certainly one of the more unique waterfalls in the region, this two tiered falls passes through two natural, moss-covered arches before plunging into the Lewis River.

The arches were formed when the waters of Curly Creek carved a path through an ancient lava tube. Lava tubes are abundant in the area, and are formed when still-hot, flowing lava below carves its way through already cooled lava above.

Since the falls is located on the opposite side of the canyon, photographers will want to use a telephoto lens in the range of 100mm to 300mm.

51

BIG CREEK FALLS

Location: Gifford Pinchot National Forest

Maps: USGS–Burnt Creek

Stream: Big Creek

Round Trip Hike Distance: 0.25 mile

Difficulty: Easy

Height: 110 feet

Volume: Medium

Best Season: Spring, summer, fall

SPECIAL NOTES: A Northwest Forest Pass is required to park at the trailhead, and is available at all ranger stations as well as many private vendors. Caution should be used when approaching the steep drop-offs overlooking the falls.

DIRECTIONS: From Woodland, travel on SR 503 east, following the signs to Mount St. Helens and Cougar. As you pass through the small town of Cougar, SR 503 turns into County Road 90. After you have traveled 38.5 miles from Woodland, follow the signs to Carson as County Road 90 veers to the right just past the Pine Creek ranger station. Continue on County Road 90 for another 9 miles to the signed trailhead.

THE FALLS: From the parking area, a short fern-lined interpretive trail leads through an old-growth stand of Douglas fir and hemlock draped in moss. Signboards along the trail tell about the formation of old-growth forests and the diversity contained within them. Soon the trail leads to a rocky precipice overlooking the 110-foot-high falls. Here Big Creek plunges over an overhanging basalt cliff and into a deep, dark, circular plunge pool alongside the Lewis River. The cloud of mist boiling up from the base of the falls nourishes a thick growth of moss and ferns on the rocks behind the falls.

The afternoon hours provide the best light for photography. Contrary to the general rule, a long shutter speed seems to emphasize the power of the falls.

52

COPPER CREEK FALLS AND LEWIS RIVER FALLS

Location: Gifford Pinchot National Forest

Maps: USGS–Lewis River

Stream: Copper Creek, Lewis River

Round Trip Hike Distance: 7 miles

Difficulty: Moderate

Height: Copper Creek Falls, 200 feet; Lower Lewis Creek Falls, 60 feet; Middle Falls, 40 feet; Upper Falls, 80 feet

Volume: Copper Creek Falls, small; Lewis River Falls (all), large

Best Season: Late spring, early fall

SPECIAL NOTES: A Northwest Forest Pass is required to park at the recreation area and is available at many private vendors. The river is at its peak flow during the spring runoff; however, during this time the water is often muddy. The most scenic views of the falls are in the late spring, when the volume is still high, but the water is crystal clear.

DIRECTIONS: From Woodland, travel on SR 503 east, following the signs to Mount St. Helens and Cougar. As you pass through the small town of Cougar, SR 503 turns into County Road 90. After you have traveled 38.5 miles from Woodland, follow the signs to Carson as County Road 90 veers to the right, just past the Pine Creek ranger station. Continue on County Road 90 for another 14.5 miles to the Lewis River Recreation Area located on the right, just past the bridge crossing the Lewis River.

THE FALLS: This short 4-mile section of the Lewis River passes by five waterfalls, four of them on the Lewis River itself. Although all of the waterfalls are relatively easy to access from the road, by far the preferred way to visit and experience the falls is by the Lewis River Trail. This well-maintained 3.5-mile path takes you through old-growth Douglas fir, western red cedar, vine maple, and Oregon-grape as it winds its way along the river.

As you arrive from Cougar and cross the bridge 0.25 mile before the entrance to the Lewis River Recreation Area, you get your first glimpse of the 60-foot-high and 200-foot-wide Lower Lewis River Falls. Here, the river makes a slow turn to the west, just before tumbling over ancient basalt lava. For a closer view, turn right into the Lewis River Recreation

Lower Lewis River Falls

Area, and follow the road to the day-use parking area. From here, a gravel path leads a few hundred feet to a railed platform overlooking Lower Lewis River Falls.

From the viewing platform, Copper Creek, Middle and Upper Lewis River Falls, and Taitnapum Falls are located just upstream, along the 3.5 mile scenic trail.

To visit Copper Creek Falls and Middle Falls, which lie just 2 miles upstream, follow the gravel path along the river and past the campground. Soon the gravel gives way to the forest humus. Another 1.75 miles brings you to a small footbridge crossing Copper Creek, just downstream from the 200-foot-high Copper Creek Falls as it slides down the cliff face and into the Lewis River. A short 0.25 mile further brings you to the base of the 40-foot-high and 100-foot-wide gentle slide of Middle Lewis River Falls.

From Middle Lewis River Falls, the trail continues upstream, passing beneath an overhanging cliff carved by the river, for another 1.25 miles to Upper Lewis River Falls. You get your first glimpse of the 80-foot-high Upper Lewis River Falls after just 0.75 mile. At this point the trail crosses a small footbridge over Alec Creek, and then makes a short climb above the river, where a trail spur to the right leads to the rim of the falls. Here, flowing over ancient basalt, the Lewis River cascades down through a narrow chute before tumbling into a deep plunge pool.

For an extra treat, follow the main trail upstream another 0.25 mile, where you come to the small, 20-foot-high but very scenic Taitnapum Falls nestled among 200-foot-high Douglas fir and cedar.

If you prefer to drive, just follow County Road 90 upriver 1.5 miles to the marked pullout for Middle Lewis River Falls. A short, steep trail loop leads down past the lip of Copper Falls to the Lewis River and the base of Middle Lewis River Falls.

There is no easy road access to Upper Lewis River Falls. However, if you would like to shorten the hike, drive 2 miles upriver past the Middle Lewis River Falls parking area to the Quartz Creek bridge, and park at the pullout. Follow the trail leading downstream, where after 0.5 mile you'll pass Taitnapum Falls, and just 0.25 mile farther brings you to Upper Lewis River Falls.

53

BIG SPRING CREEK FALLS

Location: Gifford Pinchot National
Forest
Maps: USGS–Steamboat Mountain
Stream: Big Spring Creek
Round Trip Hike Distance: At

roadside
Difficulty: Easy
Height: 30 feet
Volume: Small
Best Season: Spring, summer, fall

SPECIAL NOTES: No fees or access permits are required.

DIRECTIONS: The falls is located 19.5 miles north of the small town of Trout Lake on FR 90, and just 0.25 mile before the junction with the

Big Spring Creek Falls

gravel FS 3222. A broad, unmarked parking area on the right side of the road is located near the base of the falls.

THE FALLS: Crystal-clear and fern-lined, Big Spring Creek cascades 30 feet over and through a clutter of moss-covered roots and boulders, in several small tiers. This is an exceptionally photogenic area, especially when a light dusting of snow covers the ground. Both sides of the stream are easily accessed, and photographers should plan on spending quite a bit of time here. The best light is in the late afternoon. Both macro and wide-angle lenses will be of use. A polarizing filter and warming filter are recommended.

54

DOUGAN FALLS

Location: Gifford Pinchot National Forest
Maps: USGS–Bobs Mountain
Stream: Washougal River
Round Trip Hike Distance: At roadside
Difficulty: Easy
Height: 30 feet
Volume: Large
Best Season: Spring, fall, winter

SPECIAL NOTES: During the summer months, the falls and surrounding area can become very crowded and very littered. No fees or permits are required.

DIRECTIONS: From Washougal, turn north onto SR 140 (Washougal River Road) and follow it approximately 20 miles to the Dougan Falls bridge, the second bridge crossing the river. A parking area is located just past the bridge on the right.

THE FALLS: The last in a series of waterfalls, here the Washougal River carves its way through an old basalt lava flow and tumbles 30 feet, into a deep and narrow channel. There are good views of the falls from the bridge, but the best views are from the rocks just upstream from the bridge.

Dougan Falls

55

PANTHER CREEK FALLS

Location: Gifford Pinchot National Forest

Maps: USGS–Big Huckleberry Mountain

Stream: Panther Creek

Round Trip Hike Distance: 0.25 mile

Difficulty: Easy

Height: 135 feet

Volume: Medium

Best Season: Spring, summer, fall

SPECIAL NOTES: No fees or permits are required.

DIRECTIONS: From the town of Carson, drive 6 miles north on the Wind River Road to the second turnoff for Old State Road. Turn right onto Old State Road, and then make a quick left onto Panther Creek Road. Follow Panther Creek Road 7.5 miles, staying to the right at the unmarked intersection a couple miles past the campground. An unmarked pullout in an old gravel quarry marks the parking area.

THE FALLS: The start of the short path leading down to the falls is located a few yards back down the road. The path passes through old-growth Douglas fir as it makes a switchback to meet the creek a few yards above the falls. After a brief stroll along the creek, you come to the observation platform perched on the

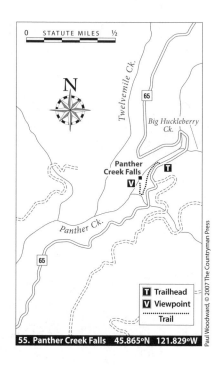

cliff just above Panther Creek Falls. The entire west fan portion of the falls is spring-fed with the water emerging just below the rim of the canyon. At the same time, the waters of Panther Creek follow a natural channel paralleling the canyon rim before tumbling over, producing a 100-foot-high horsetail.

Because of its unique shape and composition, this can be a difficult waterfall to photograph. The best view is from the observation platform and the best light is on an overcast day, or when the sun has passed below the tree line, and the entire falls is in the shade.

On your way back, take some time to watch the creek follow the channel just before it tumbles over the cliff.

Panther Creek Falls

56

HARDY FALLS AND RODNEY FALLS

Location: Columbia River Gorge National Scenic Area
Maps: USGS–Beacon Rock
Stream: Hardy Creek
Round Trip Hike Distance: 2.25 miles

Difficulty: Moderate
Height: Hardy Falls, 100 feet; Rodney Falls, 90 feet
Volume: Small
Best Season: Spring, summer, fall, winter

SPECIAL NOTES: A Washington State Parks day-use permit is required, and is available at the park entrance.

DIRECTIONS: From Vancouver, follow SR 14 east 28 miles to the signed road for the Beacon Rock State Park Campground on the left. Follow the road 0.25 mile to the trailhead for the Hamilton Mountain Trail.

THE FALLS: Native Americans called it Che-che-op-tin, "the navel of the world." Today it is known as Beacon Rock, an 848-foot-high basalt pillar that was once the throat of an ancient volcano, which draws rock climbers from around the nation.

The trail offers several views of Beacon Rock as it sets off to the two waterfalls through a second-growth Douglas fir forest. After a short distance, the trail passes under a set of power lines and the trail forks. Stay to the right, and continue along the trail as it re-enters the forest, lined with vine maple, Oregon-

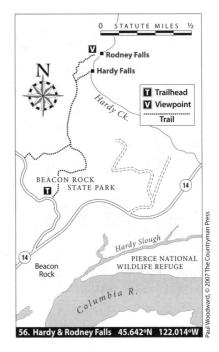

56. Hardy & Rodney Falls   45.642°N   122.014°W

Paul Woodward, © 2007 The Countryman Press

grape, and sword fern. After a short 0.5 mile, a spur trail to the right leads to a obscured view of Hardy Falls. This 100-foot-high cascade plunges down an exposed rock face covered in a thick growth of moss.

Continue along the main trail for another few hundred yards, and then follow the short side trail to the left that leads to a protected viewpoint beside Rodney Falls, where Hardy Creek drops 40 feet into a deep, narrow rock bowl, named the "Pool of the Winds." From the pool, the creek makes a second 50-foot drop, through a narrow crack in the bowl, onto the rock below. Continue along the main trail for another few hundred feet, to the bridge at the base of the falls.

III. Oregon Cascades

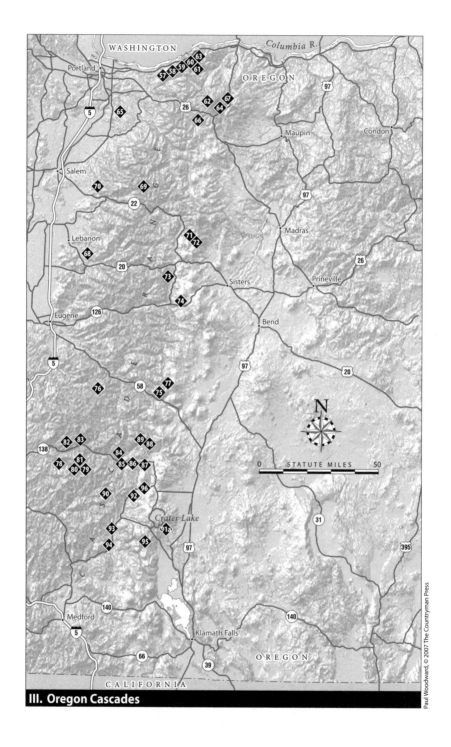

INTRODUCTION

The largest geological feature in the state, the Oregon Cascades run from the California border in the south to the Columbia River in the north. It divides the state into the relatively low and wet western valleys, and the high eastern desert—the highly populated liberal west from the sparsely populated conservative east.

The Cascades are a relatively young mountain range with most of the high peaks dating back less than 1 million years. The range is also still quite active, as illustrated by the recent discovery of a slight uplift occurring just west of South Sister.

The Cascades are home to Oregon's only national park, Crater Lake, and 20 wilderness areas ranging in size from the largest (Three Sisters at 285,202 acres) to the smallest (Menagerie at 5,033 acres). Although thousands of hikers head into the Cascades each year, due to the size of the region these sites still remain relatively unpopulated, and it is still possible to find areas of complete solitude.

Climate

The climate of the Cascades is very diverse. The high-elevation western slopes receive nearly 100 inches of precipitation annually, while the eastern slopes may receive as little as 15 inches annually. The lower trails, below 4,000 feet, are usually free of snow from May until October. The upper trails usually clear by mid-June and are open until September, although snow is possible in the highest elevations year round. Summer temperatures in the higher elevations are typically in the 60s or 70s in the day, but can easily drop below freezing at night. Temperatures in the lower elevations are roughly 5 to 10 degrees warmer.

Precautions

Many of the trails in the book pass by steep cliffs and rushing whitewater, and in many instances the edge can be unstable and/or slippery. Stay on the trails in these areas and refrain from climbing over fences and railings.

When hiking at high elevations, even on short trails, it is important to carry extra water and to take your time.

Weather can change without warning, and snow is possible during any season. If your travels take you over mountain passes, make sure to check conditions before setting out.

Attractions

- Even if you are not a skier, the Timberline Lodge National Historic Landmark is worth visiting. Completed in 1938 by the federal Works Projects Administration (WPA) it is perched just above the timberline at 6,000 feet and offers spectacular views south to Mount Jefferson. The lodge was built entirely by hand, inside and out, by unemployed craftspeople and contains some truly spectacular iron- and masonry-work.

- Located at the summit of McKenzie Pass on McKenzie Highway (OR 242) is the Dee Wright Observatory, a stone memorial named for the Civilian Conservation Corps foreman who oversaw the highway's construction. Built in the 1930s by the CCC, the highway offers panoramic views of the Cascade Mountain Range as far north as Mount Hood. A bronze "peak finder" plaque in the observatory points to the geologic features in the lava fields surrounding the observatory.

- Theodore Roosevelt signed legislation creating Oregon's first national park and the nation's fifth national park, Crater Lake, in 1902. Its hypnotizing blue waters, a result of its great depth and clarity, belie the cataclysmic forces that created the lake 7,700 years ago. The once 12,000-foot-high peak of Mount Mazama began a series of large eruptions 7,700 years ago, ejecting 13 cubic miles of the mountain and creating the 4,000-foot-deep caldera. As the eruptions subsided, rain and snowmelt gradually filled the caldera. Today the depth of the lake is 1,958 feet, making it the deepest lake in the United States, and the seventh deepest lake in the world.

- The Oregon Caves National Monument is located 20 miles east of Cave Junction, on OR 46. Located below some of the largest Douglas fir trees in the state are 3.5 miles of marble caverns, the remnants of 190-million-year-old Pacific reefs. The caverns contain one of the largest populations of endemic cave-dwelling insects in the United States. It has also recently gained fame for the discovery of a Pleistocene Age jaguar and grizzly bear fossils. Guided tours are offered from March through November and explore a 0.5 mile section of the underground world.

57

LATOURELL FALLS

Location: Columbia River Gorge
National Scenic Area
Maps: USGS–Bridal Veil
Stream: Latourell Creek
Round Trip Hike Distance:
Latourell Falls, at roadside; Upper
Latourell Falls, 2.25 miles

Difficulty: Easy to moderate
Height: Latourell Falls, 249 feet;
Upper Latourell Falls, 125 feet
Volume: Medium
Best Season: Spring, summer, fall,
winter

SPECIAL NOTES: No fees or permits are required. Latourell Falls is wheelchair accessible.

DIRECTIONS: From Portland, drive 28 miles east on I-84 to Exit 28 (Bridal Veil). Follow the Columbia River Scenic Highway west 2.75 miles, to the Latourell Falls parking area.

THE FALLS: A short, paved path leads a few hundred feet up to a viewpoint overlooking this spectacular falls, as it plunges 249 feet over an overhanging basalt cliff covered in yellow lichen. To get a better view of the falls, follow the paved path leading upstream along the creek to the base of the falls, where it plunges into a deep pool. A fine mist continually blows across the trail, so photographers will want to bring protection for their equipment. In windy conditions the falls is blown from side to side, producing a truly dramatic performance.

To reach Upper Latourell Falls, follow the trail up past the viewpoint. From here, the pavement ends and the trail climbs steeply up the cliff to a viewpoint overlooking Latourell Falls. Just past the viewpoint the trail forks. Follow the left path as it follows the creek through alder, maple,

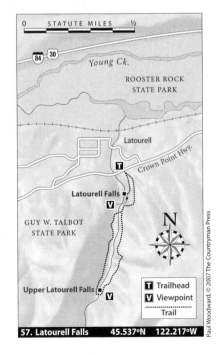

Latourell Falls

and fir. In the spring, orange salmonberries provide a sweet trailside snack. After another relatively level mile, the trail reaches the base of Upper Latourell Falls as it corkscrews 125 feet down a basalt outcropping. A footbridge crosses just in front of the falls, but the best view of the falls is from the trail a hundred yards before the bridge.

The trail makes a loop, so you have the option of either backtracking to the parking area, or continuing along the loop, which provides several views of the Columbia River Gorge on your way back to the parking area. The loop adds an additional 0.5 mile to the hike.

58

WAHKEENA FALLS AND MULTNOMAH FALLS

Location: Columbia River Gorge National Scenic Area

Maps: USGS–Multnomah Falls, Bridal Veil

Stream: Wahkeena Creek, Multnomah Creek

Round Trip Hike Distance:

Wahkeena Falls, at roadside; Multnomah Falls, 5.25 miles

Difficulty: Easy to moderate

Height: 20–621 feet

Volume: Small, medium

Best Season: Spring, summer, fall, winter

SPECIAL NOTES: No fees or permits are required. The lower sections of both waterfalls are wheelchair accessible. During the winter months ice can coat the upper portion of the Multnomah Falls Trail, making it extremely dangerous.

DIRECTIONS: From Portland, drive 28 miles east on I-84 to Exit 28 (Bridal Veil). Follow the Historic Columbia River Scenic Highway east 2.75 miles to the Wahkeena Falls Trail parking area on the right. The Multnomah Falls parking area and lodge is located 0.5 mile farther along the highway.

THE FALLS: Multnomah Falls is the single most visited scenic attraction in the state of Oregon. On average, 1.5 million people visit the falls each year. However, the vast majority of these visitors stay near the gift shop or only hike the lower portion of the trails, leaving the upper sections relatively unoccupied.

As you travel east along the Historic Columbia River Highway, Wahkeena Falls is the first major roadside waterfall encountered. The view from the parking area is exceptionally scenic in the fall. With the waterfall and

Multnomah Falls

stone footbridge in the background, Wahkeena Creek tumbles down a
rock-strewn creekbed lined with maple trees. A paved trail begins at the
west end of the Wahkeena Falls parking area and gradually climbs through
the typical flora of the Columbia Gorge including maple, Douglas fir, and
sword fern for 0.25 mile, to a moss-covered stone footbridge at the base

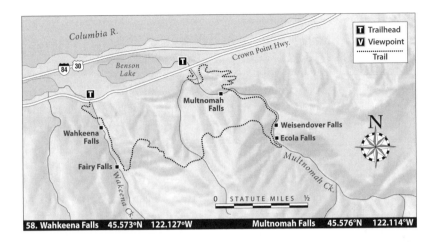

of the falls. The falls itself is a series of smaller cascades totaling 240 feet that makes its way through a narrow, winding chute of moss-covered basalt.

From the footbridge, the pavement ends as the trail continues to climb. After 0.5 mile, the trail forks. The left fork leads down to Multnomah Falls along the Perdition Trail, while the right fork leads to Fairy Falls. Following the right fork, the trail continues its climb for another 0.5 mile, before encountering two short spurs that lead to Lemon's and Monument Viewpoints, overlooking the Columbia River Gorge. The main trail soon rejoins and twice crosses Wahkeena Creek as it passes through the steep canyon for another mile, before reaching the 20-foot-high fan of Fairy Falls, cascading down a small section of columnar basalt lined with moss and ferns.

Continuing on for a few hundred feet more, the trail encounters the lower junction of the Vista Point Trail. Stay to the right, where in a little more than 0.25 mile, the trail arrives at the Angels Rest Trail junction. Turn left, and after another 0.25 mile, the trail passes two more junctions; stay right at the first (upper junction of the Vista Point Trail) and left at the second (Devils Rest Trail).

From here, the trail levels off and provides glimpses of the Columbia River 1,500 feet below. In the spring, wildflowers are abundant along various sections of the trail. Trillium, glacier lilies, and blue camas bloom in the early spring, and are followed by columbine, candy flower, bleeding heart, foxglove, and tiger lilies.

After 1 mile, the trail reaches Multnomah Creek and the junction to the Larch Mountain Trail. Turn left and follow the path downstream, where you soon come to Ecola Falls, a 50-foot-high curtain that plunges over a basalt precipice and into a small clear pool. A short distance further, the trail passes yet another basalt ledge and the 50-foot-high Weisendanger Falls, as it plunges into a deep moss-lined pool.

Continuing along, the trail passes through Dutchman's Tunnel, a basalt overhang. Just below Dutchman's Tunnel, the trail passes a series of small 5- to 10-foot-high cascades, commonly referred to as Dutchman Falls. From here, it's just a few hundred feet to the brink of the upper tier of Multnomah Falls. The highest waterfall in the state of Oregon, it is a two-tiered falls totaling 611 feet. The first section is 542 feet high and the second section, which passes under the signature stone bridge, falls another 69 feet.

From the Multnomah Falls upper viewpoint, it's a relatively steep descent on a paved trail for the next mile to the historic Multnomah Falls Lodge. Take your time on the way down, not only to absorb the power and beauty of these falls, but also to look closely at the cliff behind the falls, which is composed of six separate flows of Columbia River basalt that date from 6 to 15 million years ago.

The falls and the surrounding 300 acres were originally owned by Simon Benson, who in 1914 commissioned Italian stone masons to construct the bridge between the upper and lower falls. In 1915, he donated the land to the City of Portland. In 1925 the city built the lodge, which contains every type of rock found in the gorge, at the then-exorbitant cost of $40,000. In 1981, the lodge was listed on the National Register of Historic Places.

Photographers will want to bring all of their equipment, especially if they are planning on hiking the full loop. Late afternoon provides the best light for Multnomah Falls. The other falls along the trail are in the shade for the greater portion of the day.

59

TRIPLE FALLS, PONYTAIL FALLS, AND HORSETAIL FALLS

Location: Columbia River Gorge National Scenic Area

Maps: USGS–Multnomah Falls, USFS–Trails of the Columbia Gorge

Stream: Oneonta Creek

Round Trip Hike Distance: Triple Falls, 4.5 miles; Ponytail Falls, 0.5 mile, Horsetail Falls, at roadside

Difficulty: Moderate

Height: Triple Falls, 130 feet; Ponytail Falls, 80 Feet; Horsetail Falls, 130 Feet

Volume: Medium

Best Season: Spring, summer, fall, winter

SPECIAL NOTES: While the lower portions of the trail can be busy during spring and summer weekends, the section along Oneonta Gorge and Triple Falls is usually much less populated.

DIRECTIONS: From Portland, drive 35 miles east on I-84 to Exit 35 (Ainsworth State Park). Follow the Columbia River Scenic Highway 1.5 miles to the Horsetail Falls Trail parking area on the right. From Hood River, take Exit 35 (Ainsworth State Park) and follow the Historic Columbia River Scenic Highway 1.5 miles to Horsetail Falls.

Triple Falls

THE FALLS: The Triple Falls Trail offers spectacular vistas of the Columbia River, passes behind a waterfall, and peers into a hidden moss-covered gorge.

True to its name, Horsetail Falls twists 130 feet down a shallow channel that it has carved into the basalt cliff. The falls is located just off the Historic Columbia River Scenic Highway, and the plunge pool is partially surrounded by stonework that was constructed during the building of this road.

The trail up to Triple Falls begins just east of Horsetail Falls, at the Ponytail Falls trailhead. After climbing 0.25 mile through a few switchbacks, the trail leads behind 80-foot-high Ponytail Falls. The cave behind the falls was created by the fall's old splash pool, which washed away the softer sediment buried underneath one of the many lava flows of the area.

Continuing on for another 0.5 mile through cedar and Douglas fir will bring you to a fork; stay to the left, where after another 0.5 mile the trail switchbacks down Oneonta Gorge to the bridge looking onto 60-foot Oneonta Falls. From here, a short climb of a few hundred feet brings you to the junction with the Oneonta Trail. Turn left, and follow the trail a relatively steep 0.75 miles to the Triple Falls viewpoint.

The best and most photogenic view of Triple Falls is from the viewpoint, 0.75 mile up the trail. From here, the three chutes of the 130-foot falls are framed by the maple trees that overhang the creek. Another 0.25 mile brings you to the bridge crossing the creek just above the falls. This is a good place to stop, rest, and have lunch.

On your return trip, you can either backtrack down Ponytail Falls Trail or take the Oneonta Gorge Trail back to the highway where, after 0.5 mile, it will lead you back to the Horsetail Falls parking area. It's roughly the same distance either route you choose.

In the summer, you may want to put on some shorts and sandals and hike into Oneonta Gorge. The low water levels of summer and the early fall months provide the opportu-

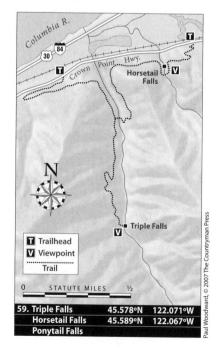

| Trailhead | Viewpoint | Trail |

0   STATUTE MILES   ½

59. Triple Falls	45.578°N	122.071°W
Horsetail Falls	45.589°N	122.067°W
Ponytail Falls		

Paul Woodward, © 2007 The Countryman Press

nity for a hike into the gorge. The cold, clear water of the creek covers the floor wall to wall, but never gets more than waist deep. After approximately 0.5 mile you come to the spectacular 100-foot-high Oneonta Gorge Falls.

60

WAHCLELLA FALLS

Location: Columbia River Gorge National Scenic Area
Maps: USGS–Bonneville Dam and Tanner Butte, USFS–Trails of the Columbia Gorge
Stream: Tanner Creek
Round Trip Hike Distance: 1.75 miles
Difficulty: Easy
Height: 90 feet
Volume: Medium
Best Season: Spring, summer, fall, winter

SPECIAL NOTES: A Northwest Forest Pass is required to park at the trailhead and is available at ranger stations and many private vendors.

DIRECTIONS: From Portland, travel east 40 miles on I-84 and take Exit 40 (Bonneville Dam). Turn right (opposite the dam), and follow the road along Tanner Creek for a few hundred feet to the parking lot. From Hood River, travel west 20 miles on I-84 to Exit 40, turn left under I-84, and follow the road along Tanner Creek for a few hundred feet to the parking lot.

THE FALLS: The trail and adjacent Bonneville Dam make for a great family outing. The manicured grounds at the Bonneville Dam Fish Hatchery have a very nice picnic area, and the hatchery offers self-guided tours of the salmon incubators and rearing ponds. Water from Tanner Creek is diverted into several ponds, where you can feed large rainbow trout and view 10-foot-long, 600-pound white sturgeon.

The cool air and refreshing mist near the falls' plunge pool makes this a nice short hike on hot summer days. However, during times of high runoff, this 90-foot-high falls can be a thunderous experience.

The trail begins by following Tanner Creek along a gravel service road for 0.25 mile to a small diversion dam for the Bonneville fish hatchery. From here, the trail crosses a small footbridge that passes below a small seasonal cascade, which can be quite spectacular with heavy runoff.

The trail continues through bigleaf maple and Douglas fir and along the creek, where you are almost certain to get a glimpse of American dippers feeding in the swift waters.

Although somewhat rare, during the spring and early summer you may

Wahclella Falls

glimpse a harlequin duck. During much of the year, harlequins are found along the coast on offshore sea stacks, or in bays and estuaries. However, during the breeding season they nest on rocks or fallen trees along mountain streams. Their feeding habits are similar to that of the dipper—diving to the bottom and walking along the streambed by holding onto rocks, in search of aquatic food.

After 0.75 mile, the trail forks; stay to the left, and after another 0.25 mile you will come to the plunge pool of Wahclella Falls. The 90-foot falls is two-tiered, with the top section plunging into a narrow slot, and a small pool which spills out for the final 60-foot drop.

The trail continues across a footbridge, just below the plunge pool, to the other side of the creek, and under a deep overhang of the surrounding basalt cliffs. In 1973, this was the site of a landslide which brought down the rubble and house-sized boulders present on this side of the creek; a small reminder that mother nature isn't yet finished sculpting the landscape.

The trail continues for another few hundred yards, where it again crosses Tanner Creek and rejoins the trail at the previous fork.

The majority of the upper tier is obscured by the basalt cliff. The best views of the lower tier are from the bridge or the large boulder on the east side of the creek, just in front of the plunge pool. To get a good view of the bridge and the falls, scramble partway up the slide on the west side of the creek.

61

ELOWAH FALLS AND UPPER MCCORD CREEK FALLS

Location: Columbia River Gorge National Scenic Area
Maps: USGS–Tanner Butte
Stream: McCord Creek
Round Trip Hike Distance: 3 miles

Difficulty: Easy
Height: Elowah Falls, 289 feet; Upper McCord Creek Falls, 80 feet
Volume: Medium
Best Season: Spring, summer, fall, winter

SPECIAL NOTES: A Northwest Forest Pass is required to park at the trailhead, and is available at ranger stations and many private vendors. Due to the steep cliffs, the upper trail is not recommended for small children.

DIRECTIONS: From Portland, travel east 35 miles on I-84 and take Exit 35 signed for Ainsworth State Park. Turn left, and after a few hundred feet, make a sharp right onto Frontage Road. Follow Frontage Road for a little more than 2 miles to John B. Yeon State Park.

THE FALLS: From the parking area, follow the Elowah Falls trail up through the fir and hemlock, where after 0.3 mile the trail forks. Stay to the left at the trail junction, and after another 0.5 mile the trail crosses McCord Creek at the end of a large amphitheater, just below the base of

289-foot-high Elowah Falls. McCord Creek plunges over ancient basalt lava flows covered with bright yellow lichen and down into a small, crystal-clear plunge pool.

To get a view of the falls from the rim of the amphitheater and to view Upper McCord Creek Falls, backtrack to the trail junction and turn left. The trail switchbacks up steeply for 0.3 mile to a railed viewpoint, carved from the cliff and overlooking the falls. Continue along the trail another 0.25 mile to reach the viewpoint for the 80-foot-high falls. The waterfall is composed of two segments cascading over a lush green basalt bluff and onto the rocks below.

An overcast day or late afternoon provides the best light for photography. Wide-angle lenses and a polarizing filter are recommended.

62

RAMONA FALLS

Location: Mount Hood National Forest
Maps: USGS–Bull Run Lake, USFS–Mount Hood Wilderness Area
Stream: Ramona Creek
Round Trip Hike Distance: 7 miles
Difficulty: Moderate
Height: 120 feet
Volume: Medium
Best Season: Late spring, summer, early fall

SPECIAL NOTES: The temporary footbridge over the Sandy River is in place from April to October. A Northwest Forest Pass is required to park at the trailhead, and is available at ranger stations and from many private vendors.

DIRECTIONS: From Portland, drive 40 miles east on US 26 to Zigzag. Turn left onto Lolo Pass Road, and follow it 5 miles to FS 1825. Turn onto FS 1825, and follow it for 2.75 miles, across the Sandy River bridge, to spur road 1825-100. Turn left onto 1825-100 and follow it to its end at the trailhead.

THE FALLS: The trail starts by following the alder and Douglas fir–lined Sandy River. The Sandy is a glacial stream, which begins at the Reid and Sandy Glaciers located only a few miles upstream. The river's milky color is due to the presence of glacial silt produced by the tremendous weight of the glaciers grinding the rock into a fine powder. The powder is then washed downstream by the melting waters.

After 1.25 miles, the trail crosses the Sandy over a seasonal bridge, put in place by the National Forest Service each spring and removed each fall. Almost immediately after crossing the seasonal bridge you come to the first trail junction. The left fork of the trail is a horse path that we'll use for the return trip; turn right instead, and after a few hundred yards you will cross Ramona Creek. Another 0.5 mile brings you to the Muddy Fork of the Sandy River, and another junction. Turn right, and head another 0.5 mile, through fir and (in the spring), beautiful pink and red rhododendron; this brings you back to the mossy rocks of Ramona Creek. From here, the falls is only a mile away.

Ramona Falls is 120 feet high, and cascades over a columnar basalt lava flow that, in part, forms the base of Mount Hood's volcanic cone. The flow dates back to between 500,000 years to 700,000 years. Sunlight filtering down through the trees can make it difficult to obtain the correct exposure for the overall scene. However, it can also produce some interesting effects as the light hits the water cascading down the moss-covered basalt.

On the return trip you can either backtrack the way you came, or continue the loop by turning right and crossing the creek. After 0.5 mile, the trail rejoins the Sandy River, which it then parallels 2 miles back to the seasonal bridge.

The last major eruption of Mount Hood occurred in 1790, during a period of activity known as the "Old Maid eruptive period." The

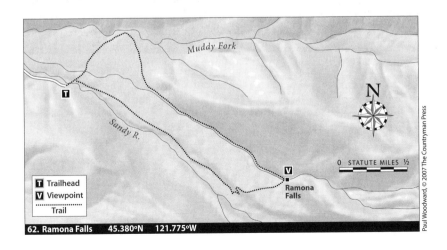

Muddy Fork

N

Sandy R.

0 STATUTE MILES ½

Ramona Falls

T Trailhead
V Viewpoint
.... Trail

62. Ramona Falls   45.380°N   121.775°W

Paul Woodward, © 2007 The Countryman Press

Ramona Falls

eruptions produced several mud flows. The evidence of one of these flows can still be seen as the stunted growth of the forest you encountered along the trail.

63

EAGLE CREEK

Location: Columbia River Gorge
National Scenic Area
Maps: USGS–Bonneville Dam,
Tanner Butte, and Wahtum Lake
Stream: Eagle Creek, Loowit
Creek, Eagle Creek (East Fork)

Round Trip Hike Distance: 12.5
miles
Difficulty: Difficult
Height: 30–120 feet
Volume: Large
Best Season: Spring, summer, fall

SPECIAL NOTES: Located only 40 minutes from Portland, this trail is extremely busy during the spring and summer months. Due to the trail's path along numerous cliffs, this route is not recommended for young children. A Northwest Forest Pass is required to park at the trailhead, and is available at ranger stations and from many private vendors.

DIRECTIONS: From Portland, travel east 41 miles on I-84 to Exit 41 (Eagle Creek). Turn right at the hatchery building, and follow Eagle Creek Road 0.5 mile to the trailhead. Since there is no westbound exit from Hood River, take Exit 40 (Bonneville Dam) and double back on I-84 to the Eagle Creek exit.

THE TRAIL: Built in the 1910s to complement the then-new Columbia River Highway, Eagle Creek is one of the most spectacular trails in the entire Northwest. In places, the trail is precariously cut into the basalt cliffs high above the creek, and passes five major waterfalls.

The trail begins at the south end of the parking area along Eagle Creek and follows it through western cedar, Douglas fir, and bigleaf maple. It soon begins climbing up the moss-covered basalt canyon walls, and after 0.75 of a mile you reach the first of several cliffs to be traversed. A cable handrail

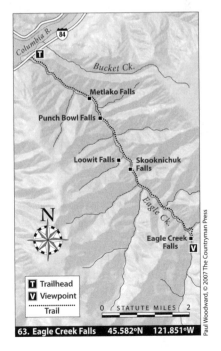

63. Eagle Creek Falls 45.582°N 121.851°W

Paul Woodward, © 2007 The Countryman Press

Metlako Falls

is mounted on the inside cliff wall, and provides some sense of security. Another 0.75 of a mile brings you to a junction with a short trail spur to the right, which leads to a viewpoint for the 100-foot-high Metlako Falls, the first of the five major falls along the trail. The falls plunge from a basalt overhang and into a large, deep pool. With the leaves fallen from the trees, the winter months provide the best view from this distant viewpoint. Spring and summer vegetation provides an almost fairy-tale appearance.

Continuing along the main trail for another 0.25 mile, the trail reaches the junction for Punch Bowl Falls. The main trail continues to the left, while to the right a short trail spur leads 0.25 mile to a rocky beach just downstream from the falls. This view of the 30-foot-high falls is the best known, and certainly the most photographed, view of the falls. Although the view is still very photogenic, a large Douglas fir has fallen into the narrow gorge of the splash pool, partially obstructing the view for the past several years. This waterfall is the true definition of a "punchbowl," as it plunges through a small chute carved into the moss-covered basalt and into a huge, deep pool. Another 0.25 mile along the main trail through brings you to the Punch Bowl Falls overlook. The overlook provides a beautiful view looking down onto the falls and punchbowl.

From here, the trail climbs slightly through old-growth fir and cedar. Along the trail, look for trillium, monkeyflower, wild iris, and the occasional avalanche lily. After a mile, you come to the most nerve-racking portion of the trail, as it passes along the Eagle Creek gorge and onto High Bridge, which then crosses the gorge. Here the trail is carved along the side of the gorge, 120 feet above the roaring waters below. Hold onto the cable handrail and look across the gorge for Loowit Falls as it cascades into Eagle Creek. This lacey waterfall of Loowit Creek is 60 feet high, and is best viewed in the spring. In the late summer months it is reduced to a small trickle.

About 0.25 mile past High Bridge is the broad, 50-foot-high Skoonichuk Falls. It is difficult to get a good view of this two-tiered punchbowl without risking life or limb. A short trail spur on the left leads to the top of the falls.

From here, the trail is at creek level and follows it for another 0.75 mile, where it crosses the creek on a footbridge bringing you to the Wy'east Backpacking Camp. At the 5-mile mark the trail again forks. The left fork leads to the Benson Plateau and the Pacific Crest Trail. Take the right fork to the Blue Grouse Camp, just 0.25 mile away. Along the way, watch for American dippers diving into the creek, looking for food.

If you are planning on camping at any of the camping areas, it is best to arrive on a weekday or very early. Camping is only allowed in the designated areas and, with limited space, they fill up quick during the summer months. Check at the Eagle Creek Ranger Station for any additional regulations.

From the Blue Grouse Camp, the trail once again begins to climb the walls of the canyon. After 0.75 of a mile you come to the 120-foot-high Tunnel Falls. The name becomes obvious as the trail leads up to, and then behind, the falls through a tunnel carved into the basalt. It's a truly unique experience to pass behind the falls and emerge so close to the falling water of East Fork Eagle Creek while perched on the rocky ledge 60 feet in the air.

A few hundred yards further along, the trail leads to the top of Eagle Creek Falls as it twists 60 feet down a narrow chute. Only the top portion of the falls is visible.

This is another "must stop" for waterfall lovers and photographers. Photographers should plan on bringing all of their equipment. Overcast days, the early morning, and late afternoon hours provide the best light.

64

UMBRELLA FALLS AND SAHALIE FALLS

Location: Mount Hood National Forest

Maps: USGS–Mount Hood South

Stream: Hood River (East Fork)

Round Trip Hike Distance: Umbrella Falls, 0.5 mile;

Sahalie Falls, at roadside

Difficulty: Easy

Height: Umbrella Falls, 50 feet; Sahalie Falls, 75 feet

Volume: Small

Best Season: Spring, fall

SPECIAL NOTES: No fees or access permits are required.

DIRECTIONS: Travel east from Government Camp on US 26 to the intersection with US 35. Turn onto US 35 and follow it 6.5 miles to the exit for the Mount Hood Meadows Ski Area. To reach Sahalie Falls, turn right immediately after turning onto the road leading to the ski area, and follow the road a little less than 0.5 mile to the bridge crossing the East Fork of the Hood River. The falls is located just upstream. To reach Umbrella Falls, follow the access road 1 mile to the signed trailhead for Umbrella Falls.

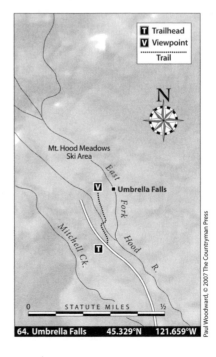

THE FALLS: Sahalie Falls crashes down a 75-foot-high rock face, tucked away in a small fir-lined dell. The best light for photography is early in the morning. A polarizing lens will help bring out the greens of the moss growing on the rock face next to the falls.

The trail leads from the Umbrella Falls parking area 0.25 mile to the base of the 50-foot-high falls, which slides down a steep rock slope. In the late summer months, the falls is reduced to little more than a trickle. However, in the spring the falls can be quite scenic, with monkeyflower and lupine blooming along the stream.

The falls is in a fairly open area, so photographers will want to arrive early in the morning in order to avoid the harsh midday light.

65

WILLAMETTE FALLS

Location: Oregon City

Maps: USGS–Oregon City

Stream: Willamette River

Round Trip Hike Distance: At roadside

Difficulty: Easy

Height: 40 feet

Volume: Very large

Best Season: Spring, summer, fall, winter

SPECIAL NOTES: No fees or permits are required.

DIRECTIONS: To reach the north viewpoint, follow I-205 north to Exit 7 and the signed scenic wayside (there is no access from I-205 southbound). To reach the south viewpoint, travel south from Oregon City on US 99E for 1.2 miles to a signed viewpoint overlooking the falls.

THE FALLS: Although it is only 40 feet high, Willamette Falls is over 1,500 feet wide, and by volume it is by far the largest waterfall in the Northwest. Native people believed that the falls was created by a great god so that their people would have fish to eat all winter, and many local tribes maintained villages in the area to harvest the abundance of salmon that were blocked from going upstream by the falls. European fur traders discovered the falls in 1810, and in 1842 Oregon City was established at the east end of the falls.

Since then the falls has undergone large-scale industrial development, beginning in 1842 with a lumber mill, then a flour mill in 1844, and a woolen mill in 1864. In 1866, the first paper mill in the northwest was built on the Oregon City side. In 1873, the Willamette Falls Locks were completed allowing small boats to navigate upstream, and a second paper mill was built in 1889 on the north side. In 1895, Portland General Electric built a small hydroelectric facility that is still in operation today, generating 14,000 kilowatts of power.

Even with this assault of industrialization, this waterfall is still impressive. The Willamette still kicks up a cloud of mist as it crashes over the basalt "bluff" which snakes its way across the river.

66

YOCUM FALLS

Location: Mount Hood National Forest

Maps: USGS–Government Camp

Stream: Camp Creek

Round Trip Hike Distance: 1 mile

Difficulty: Easy

Height: 100 feet

Volume: Medium

Best Season: Spring, summer, fall

SPECIAL NOTES: No fees or permits are required.

DIRECTIONS: From Rhododendron, head east on US 26 for 7 miles to the sno-park wayside, on the right-hand side of the road.

THE FALLS: The waterfall is located just a few yards down the Mirror Lake Trail. A narrow footbridge crosses the creek just above the falls. The waterfall slides 100 feet down an old-growth-lined chute. The best view of the falls is from back along the shoulder of the highway. The falls is named for an early entrepreneur, Oliver Yocum, who opened a hotel and resort in nearby Government Camp.

67

TAMANAWAS FALLS

Location: Mount Hood National
Forest

Maps: USGS–Dog River,
USFS–Mount Hood Wilderness
Area

Stream: Cold Spring Creek

Round Trip Hike Distance: 3.75
miles

Difficulty: Moderate

Height: 100 feet

Volume: Medium

Best Season: Spring, summer, fall

SPECIAL NOTES: Due to its length and easy access, this great family trail can become crowded during the summer months. A Northwest Forest Pass is required to park at the trailhead and is available from ranger stations and many private vendors.

DIRECTIONS: From Portland, drive 55 miles east on US 26 to the intersection with OR 35. Follow OR 35 north 18 miles, to the well-marked East Fork trailhead on the left. From Hood River, travel south on OR 35 for 23 miles and look for the East Fork trailhead on your right, 0.25 mile north of Sherwood Campground.

THE FALLS: Tamanawas Falls makes for a great summer hike. The shaded trail winds back and forth over the aptly named Cold Spring Creek, providing a welcome break from the heat of midsummer days.

The trail begins at the northwest end of the parking area where, after a few hundred yards, you cross the milky, glacial waters of the East Fork of the Hood River and turn right onto the East Fork Trail. The trail loosely follows the river, through Douglas fir and western hemlock. After 0.5 mile, turn left at the fork and cross the footbridge over Cold Spring Creek. This 1 mile section of the trail follows the creek, and has several access areas to stop and enjoy the cold water as it tumbles over the moss-covered rocks.

Stay left at the last fork, and once again cross the creek. Tamanawas Falls lies 0.5 mile ahead. The falls itself is a 100-foot-high broad curtain, which tumbles through a notch carved into the lip of an old basalt lava flow.

Take some time on the way back to look for fairy slipper, tiger lily, and twinflower that are common along the trail in the spring. Steller's jays, Clark's nutcrackers, American dippers, and golden-mantled ground squirrels all populate the area as well.

At the base of Tamanawas Falls

There are great views of the falls from the trail as you approach. However, if you are photographing, make the effort to scramble down to the rocks below the falls. Wonderful images can be obtained of the creek as it tumbles through the moss-covered boulders with the falls in the background.

68

MCDOWELL CREEK FALLS

Location: McDowell Creek
County Park
Maps: USGS–Sweet Home
Stream: McDowell Creek, Fall
Creek
Round Trip Hike Distance: 1.5

miles
Difficulty: Easy
Height: 20–119 feet
Volume: Small
Best Season: Spring, summer, fall,
winter

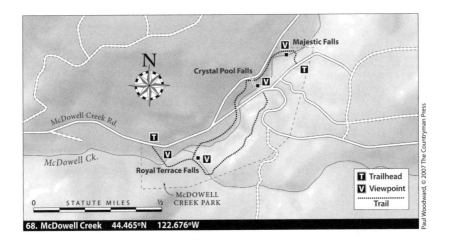

Majestic Falls

Crystal Pool Falls

McDowell Creek Rd

McDowell Ck.

Royal Terrace Falls

McDOWELL CREEK PARK

0 STATUTE MILES ½

T Trailhead
V Viewpoint
Trail

68. McDowell Creek   44.465°N   122.676°W

Paul Woodward, © 2007 The Countryman Press

SPECIAL NOTES: No fees or permits are required.

DIRECTIONS: From Lebanon, follow US 20 for 4.5 miles to Fairview Road, and follow it 2 miles to McDowell Creek Road. Follow McDowell Creek Road 3 miles to the park.

THE FALLS: The trail to Lower McDowell Creek Falls and Royal Terrace Falls begins at the first parking and picnic area. After a few hundred yards, the trail crosses McDowell Creek on a small footbridge, just above Lower McDowell Creek Falls. A short trail spur to the right leads to the base of the broad, 25-foot-high, two-tiered slide. Continuing along the main trail, bearing right at the junction, after another 0.25 mile you reach the base of Royal Terrace Falls. When Fall Creek is running at a moderate or high flow, this is the most spectacular of the four waterfalls in the park. It drops 119 feet in two tiers, with the narrower top tier cascading into a shallow rocky pool. The creek then widens and tumbles down the second tier, which partially slides onto the rocks below.

To reach Crystal Pool Falls and Majestic Falls, backtrack down to the previous trail junction, and follow it through the Douglas fir, maple, and alder 0.3 mile, to where the trail crosses the park road. From here, the trail continues up along the creek for another few hundred yards to the base of Crystal Pool Falls. This 20-foot-high cascade tumbles down a moss-lined chute and into a small pool. Majestic Falls lies just 0.25 mile further up the trail, which climbs past Crystal Pool Falls. The fern-lined Royal Terrace Falls drops 39 feet into a small green pool. A staircase to the right leads to a large observation deck perched at the top of the falls.

If you would prefer to drive to the falls, two parking areas along the park road are located near the base of Crystal Pool Falls and Majestic Falls, making each just a short walk.

The lush forest, moss-covered trees, and fern-lined creek make this a very photogenic area. The early morning and late afternoon hours provide the best light.

69

OPAL CREEK

Location: Opal Creek Wilderness Area

Maps: USGS–Elkhorn, Battle Ax

Stream: Little North Santiam River

Round Trip Hike Distance: 6 miles

Difficulty: Moderate

Height: 30 feet

Volume: Medium

Best Season: Spring, summer, fall

SPECIAL NOTES: Jawbone Flats maintains a resident population. Respect residents' privacy by staying on the road. A Northwest Forest Pass is required to park at the trailhead and is available at ranger stations and many private vendors.

DIRECTIONS: From Salem, travel east on US 22 (North Santiam Highway) for 23 miles to the small town of Mehama. Turn left onto Little North Fork Road and follow it 15 miles, until it turns to gravel, and another 1.25 miles to the intersection of FS 2209 and FS 2207. Take the left fork (FS 2209) and follow it 6 miles to the locked gate and the start of the trailhead.

THE FALLS: The trail begins at the locked gate, and follows the dirt road above the Little North Santiam River. The road soon crosses the Gold Creek Bridge, built in 1939, and then clings to the cliffs above the river. From here, you begin to enter the old-growth forest. Many of these trees reach a height of 250 feet, and an age of between 500 and 1,000 years. These trees were once at the heart of one of the most heated environmental battles in the nation. Throughout the late 1980s and mid-1990s, environmentalists and the timber industry squared off in the forest, and in the courtroom, until Congress created the 20,300-acre Opal Creek Wilderness Area in 1996.

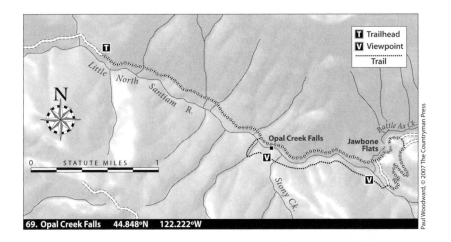

69. Opal Creek Falls   44.848°N   122.222°W

At the 2-mile mark, you will come to the remnants of the old Merten Mill, where a short trail to the right leads to the broad 30-foot Cascadia de los Ninos (Waterfall of the Children), where the Little North Santiam River cascades into a large, opalescent pool.

After another 0.25 mile, the road forks. Take the right fork, and cross the log bridge into the Opal Creek Wilderness Area, where the Opal Creek Trail begins. From here, the trail follows the river for 1.5 miles, past the 20-foot-high slide falls, to the gem-like waters of Opal Pool nestled in a scenic gorge. On the trip back, cross the bridge just above Opal Pool, follow the trail to the old mining road, and turn left to Jawbone Flats and follow the road back to the parking area.

Gold was found in the area in 1859, bringing miners from all around to try their luck. The mill produced moderate quantities of gold, silver, zinc, and lead until 1992, when it was donated by the Shiny Rock Mining Company to The Friends of Opal Creek. The camp consists of two dozen well-maintained buildings, and now acts as an old-growth forest study center.

70

SILVER FALLS

Location: Silver Falls State Park
Maps: USGS–Hamaker Butte
Stream: North Silver Creek,
South Silver Creek, Hullt Creek
Round Trip Hike Distance: At
roadside, to 7.5 miles

Difficulty: Easy to moderate
Height: 27–178 feet
Volume: Small to medium
Best Season: Spring, summer, fall,
winter

SPECIAL NOTES: An Oregon Parks day-use pass is required and is available at the entrance booth, as well as from many private vendors. The rim of South Falls is wheelchair accessible.

DIRECTIONS: From Salem, drive 10 miles east on US 22 to US 214. Travel north 15 miles on US 214, following the Silver Falls State Park signs to the park. Turn left into the South Falls/swimming area parking lot.

THE FALLS: Silver Falls State Park is not only a waterfall lover's playground, with 11 major falls along Silver Creek and its tributaries, but it is also a "must stop" for photographers in the region, or those passing through, regardless of the season. Photographers should plan on bringing all of their equipment. Overcast days, the early morning, and late afternoon hours provide the best light.

Silver Falls State Park is Oregon's largest state park, and encompasses 8,700 acres. The first European to discover the area was fur trapper Donald Mackenzie, around 1810. In the 1930s, the state began acquiring land from the region's early settlers, who had built a small mining and lumber camp named Silver Falls City. The area was officially dedicated a state park in 1933. In 1935, a CCC camp was established near North Falls, and work began on many of the park's facilities (including a boys' camp and lodge), which was listed on the National Register of Historic Places in 1983.

Beginning at the South Falls rim, viewpoints look down on the 177-foot-high falls, which plunge into a large green pool below. Follow Canyon Trail as it switchbacks down to its base and then goes behind the falls and under the basalt lava flow that provides the base for the falls. The cave was created when the softer sandstone sediments lying beneath the basalt eroded away. Approximately 25 million years ago, this area was part of the Pacific coastline. The soft sandstones evident behind many of the falls are

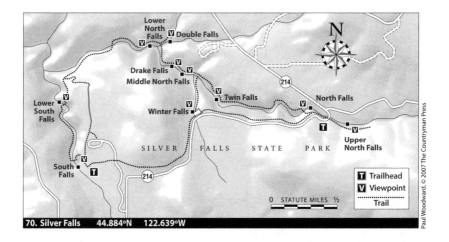

Lower
North
Falls
Double Falls

Drake Falls
Middle North Falls

Lower
South
Falls

Winter Falls

Twin Falls

North Falls

214

SILVER   FALLS   STATE   PARK

Upper
North Falls

South
Falls

214

T Trailhead

V Viewpoint

Trail

0   STATUTE MILES   ½

70. Silver Falls   44.884°N   122.639°W

Paul Woodward, © 2007 The Countryman Press

actually ancient beach sand and are part of the Scotts Mills Formation. Continental forces gradually lifted the land upward, and around 15 million years ago huge fissures in eastern Washington and Oregon erupted, resulting in the Columbia River Basalt Lava Flows that covered much of the area.

From here, the trail continues past the footbridge and along the South Fork of Silver Creek, which after another 0.75 mile brings you to a viewpoint of the 93-foot curtain of Lower South Falls as it plunges into a deep pool surrounded by ferns. The trail then crosses the creek behind the falls where, after 0.25 mile, the trail forks. For a shorter hike follow the right fork which, after 1 mile, leads up the rim and back to the South Falls parking area.

Following the Canyon Trail straight through maple, alder, and fir, it leads to the North Fork of Silver Creek. The trail crosses the creek on a small footbridge and after 0.75 mile leads to the scenic 30-foot slide of Lower North Falls. At the footbridge, just above the falls, follow the short trail to the left, which follows Hullt Creek a few hundred yards to the base of the second tier of Double Falls. This 178-foot-high delicate ribbon falls into a small amphitheater, and is the tallest of the falls in the park.

Crossing the footbridge over Hullt Creek, and following the main trail another 0.25 mile, brings you to Drake Falls, the park's smallest. A small observation deck provides a good view of the 27-foot-high slide, which is named after June Drake, an early naturalist and photographer of the area.

The next waterfall along the Canyon Trail is the 106-foot curtain of Middle North Falls, which plunges into a deep, narrow pool. A short trail to the right will lead behind the falls.

A quarter mile past Middle North Falls, the trail again forks. The hike can be made shorter by taking the Winter Falls cut-off trail to the right. Follow it across the footbridge, and up a steep 0.5 mile, to the junction of the return leg of the Canyon Trail at the top of Winter Falls. Turn right onto the Canyon Trail, and follow it back to the South Falls parking area 1.5 miles away. Follow the right fork across the footbridge, and climb the rim to the Winter Falls wayside. From here, follow the Canyon Trail back to the South Falls parking area.

Twin Falls is the next waterfall you encounter if you continue along

Upper North Falls

the Canyon Trail from Middle North Falls. It's a 31-foot-tall slide with two segments following deep channels that the creek has carved into the basalt.

From Twin Falls, it is 1 mile through moss-covered maple, alder, fir, vine maple, and ferns, to the most spectacular waterfall in the park, North Falls. Here the water has cut a single narrow channel into the basalt, leading to a dramatic 136-foot plunge onto the rocks below. The trail continues through a huge cavern behind the falls. In the basalt roof of the cave are deep circular holes. These holes are actually casts of the ancient trees living here when the lava flowed around them 15 million years ago. The wood burned away, leaving only these casts behind as evidence.

The trail then climbs steeply up the cliff next to the falls and follows the creek to another trail junction near the North Falls parking area. Take the 0.5-mile trail to the left, and follow it under the bridge to Upper North Falls, a 65-foot-high curtain that tumbles into a large pool often frequented by swimmers.

From the North Falls junction, follow the Canyon Trail along the rim 1 mile to the Winter Falls wayside. Winter Falls is a 134-foot seasonal falls. As its name implies, it is best observed in the winter months or during times of heavy runoff. From here the trail roughly parallels the park road—through second-growth fir, hemlock, and cedar with an undergrowth of Oregon-grape, salal, and ferns—1.5 miles back to the South Falls parking area.

71

GOOCH FALLS

Location: Mount Jefferson Wilderness Area

Maps: USGS–Marion Forks

Stream: Marion Creek

Round Trip Hike Distance: At roadside

Difficulty: Easy

Height: 85 feet

Volume: Large

Best Season: Spring, summer, fall

SPECIAL NOTES: A Northwest Forest Pass is required to park at the trailhead, and is available at ranger stations and many private vendors. Due to the steep, unguarded cliffs, the trail to the falls is not recommended for children.

DIRECTIONS: From Salem, drive east 66 miles on US 22 (North Santiam Highway) to Marion Forks. Turn right onto Marion Creek Road (FS 2255) and follow it 3.5 miles to FS 2255-850. Turn right onto FS 2255-850. Follow the rough dirt road for a little less than 0.25 mile to a small pullout on the right.

THE FALLS: From the parking area, a well-worn dirt path leads a hundred yards to a rock outcrop perched on the edge of the cliff, which serves as the viewpoint. From the cliff, the view extends upstream through the mist as the creek passes through a dense forest of hemlock, fir, and cedar. The creek then crashes 85 feet onto moss-covered rocks, as it plunges over a basalt cliff with a small ledge halfway down its face.

72

MARION FALLS

Location: Mount Jefferson
Wilderness Area
Maps: USGS–Marion Lake
Stream: Marion Creek
Round Trip Hike Distance: 5.75

miles
Difficulty: Moderate
Height: 140 feet
Volume: Large
Best Season: Spring, summer, fall

SPECIAL NOTES: A Northwest Forest Pass is required to park at the trailhead and is available at ranger stations and many private vendors. Due to the steep, unguarded cliffs, the trail to the falls is not recommended for children.

DIRECTIONS: From Salem, drive east 66 miles on US 22 (North Santiam Highway) to Marion Forks. Turn right onto Marion Creek Road (FS 2255) and follow it 5.5 miles to its end at the trailhead.

THE FALLS: This broad, well-traveled trail begins by passing through a thick forest of Douglas fir and hemlock. It then climbs gently for 2 miles, where it passes by the rocky shores of Lake Ann. A quarter mile past Lake Ann, the trail forks; take the trail leading to the right, where after a few hundred yards an unmarked trail spur to the right leads to the cliffside viewpoint at the top of the falls. A short, rough trail to the left leads to a better view of the 140-foot, two-tiered falls as it plunges into a small, turbulent pool below.

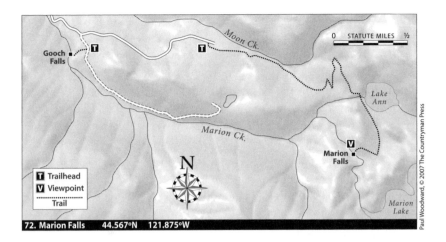

Due to the lack of a clear, unobstructed view, this is a difficult waterfall to photograph, so it is best to try and incorporate the surrounding vegetation in your composition.

73

SAHALIE FALLS AND KOOSAH FALLS

Location: Willamette National Forest

Maps: USGS–Clear Lake

Stream: McKenzie River

Round Trip Hike Distance: Sahalie Falls, 0.25 mile; Koosah Falls, 2.5 miles

Difficulty: Easy

Height: Sahalie Falls, 100 feet; Koosah Falls, 80 feet

Volume: Large

Best Season: Spring, summer, fall, winter

SPECIAL NOTES: This short trail takes you past two very different waterfalls, and through an example of Oregon's dense rainforest. The waterfalls are at their highest flow in the spring. Due to its length and easy access, sections of the trail around Sahalie Falls can become crowded during the summer months. No permits or fees are required.

DIRECTIONS: From Eugene, travel east on US 126 to McKenzie

Bridge. Continue east through McKenzie Bridge 19 miles on US 126 to the Sahalie Falls rest area on the left.

THE FALLS: Cascading over moss-covered lava, the McKenzie River creates an atmosphere that seems to briefly take you back in time.

The trail begins on the east side of the parking area; stay to the right and follow the trail 0.25 mile to a railed viewpoint at the lip of the falls. From here, you can witness the McKenzie River rush by your feet, and plunge 100 feet to the moss-covered rocks below. From here, retrace your steps and turn right at the junction where you soon come to the misty lower viewpoint. At this point you can better see the basalt lava flow that, a little more than 6,000 years ago, squeezed the river into this narrow channel.

This is also the best place to photograph the falls. Don't forget to include the moss-covered logs in the foreground, and at least some portion of the McKenzie as it exits the plunge pool.

If you continue along the trail, you will pass through a dense growth of large Douglas fir beside the churning, clear-blue waters of the McKenzie. American dippers can be seen feeding in the water, while woodpecker-like northern flickers can often be seen among the trees.

Just 0.5 mile down the trail from Sahalie Falls is the 80-foot-high Koosah Falls. Follow the short spur to the left down to the observation point for a great view of the falls. Unlike Sahalie Falls, Koosah Falls is a very broad curtain that plunges into a well-defined pool. If you look carefully, you can see many small springs flowing from the porous lava at the base of the falls.

If you prefer to drive to Koosah Falls, it is only 0.5 mile west on US 126 to the Koosah Falls wayside.

Sahalie Falls

74

PROXY FALLS

Location: Three Sisters
Wilderness Area, Willamette
National Forest
Maps: USGS–Linton Lake
Stream: Proxy Creek
Round Trip Hike Distance: 1.5
miles

Difficulty: Easy
Height: 125–200 feet
Volume: Low to medium
Best Season: Late spring, summer,
early fall

SPECIAL NOTES: Due to its length and easy access, this trail can become crowded during the summer months. A Northwest Forest Pass is required to park at the trailhead.

DIRECTIONS: From Eugene, travel east on US 126 to the junction of OR 242 (McKenzie Pass). After approximately 9 miles, a hiking sign and roadside parking area designate the trailhead. From Salem, travel east on US 20, and then south on US 126, to the OR 242 junction.

THE FALLS: Proxy Falls Trail is located along one of Oregon's many scenic byways, just inside the northwest border of the Three Sisters Wilderness Area. The waterfalls are at their highest flow in the spring. From the parking lot, walk to the right where the trail begins by crossing over a 4,500-year-old lava flow from cinder cones near the North Sister. The flow is composed of jumbled rocks, which are covered in moss and vine maple, which provides a splash of color in the fall. Where they can find a foothold, the occasional old-growth Douglas fir or hemlock towers above all. After crossing the lava, the trail forks. A few hun-

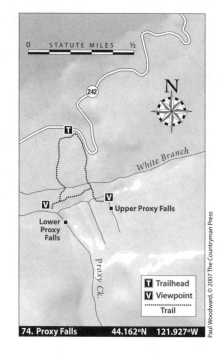

0   STATUTE MILES   ½

242

N

White Branch

Upper Proxy Falls

Lower
Proxy
Falls

Proxy Ck.

T Trailhead
V Viewpoint
Trail

74. Proxy Falls   44.162°N   121.927°W

Paul Woodward, © 2007 The Countryman Press

dred yards down the right fork, the trail ends at the Lower Proxy Falls viewpoint. Douglas fir, hemlock, and cedar trees frame the view of the falls as it cascades 200 feet down the face of the glacier-carved cliff.

Continuing along the main trail, you'll pass through old-growth western hemlock, Douglas fir, and yew trees. A spring hike will yield blooming rhododendrons, vanilla leaf, Oregon-grape, and the occasional Oregon iris. At the second fork, turn right for 0.1 mile to the smaller Upper Proxy

Lower Proxy Falls

Falls. The trail ends at the collection pool formed at the base of the 125-foot falls, which has no visible outlet. The water flows through the porous lava beneath the pool and emerges at the springs, creating Lost Creek and White Branch Creek, located several miles down the canyon.

Both upper and lower Proxy Falls cascade over basalt cliffs carved by the last Ice Age, more than 8,000 years ago.

From the upper falls collection pool, it's only a 0.5-mile hike back to the main trail, over the lava, and back to the parking lot.

75

SALT CREEK FALLS AND DIAMOND CREEK FALLS

Location: Willamette National Forest

Maps: USGS–Diamond Peak

Stream: Salt Creek, Diamond Creek

Round Trip Hike Distance: Salt Creek, 1 mile; Diamond Creek, 3.5 miles

Difficulty: Easy to moderate

Height: Salt Creek, 286 feet; Diamond Creek, 100 feet

Volume: Salt Creek, large; Diamond Creek, medium

Best Season: Late spring, summer, early fall

SPECIAL NOTES: Two very different waterfalls are highlighted in this pleasant family hike. Salt Creek Falls is an awe-inspiring show of nature's brute force, while Diamond Creek Falls displays a more delicate side. This is a very popular trail, and can become quite busy during the summer months. A Northwest Forest Pass is required to park at the trailhead, and is available at ranger stations and many private vendors.

DIRECTIONS: From Eugene, travel east on US 58. Approximately 1 mile past the tunnel, near mile post 66, look for the U.S. Forest Service sign for Salt Creek Falls on your right.

THE FALLS: At the turnaround you'll find a restroom, as well as an information booth which tells the story of the fall's creation and history. Begin the hike by stretching your legs with a little walk downstream to the overlook, which offers an impressive view of the falls from the basalt rim. At 286 feet, Salt Creek Falls is the second highest in the state behind

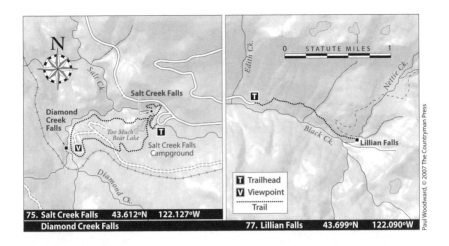

75. Salt Creek Falls 43.612°N 122.127°W
Diamond Creek Falls

77. Lillian Falls 43.699°N 122.090°W

the 542-foot Multnomah Falls. However, what it lacks in height it makes up for in volume, making it nearly as impressive as Multnomah.

The trail to the base of Salt Creek Falls begins at the far end of the overlook. From here, the trail switchbacks down just below the highway, through Douglas fir and vine maple. Along the way you will have several glimpses of the falls through the trees before you come to the trail's end, 0.5 mile later, opposite the falls and 50 feet above the large plunge pool.

If you plan to photograph from down here, bring some protection for your camera and be prepared to get wet. Although you are still 100 yards from the base of the falls, the wind generated by the falling water swirls against the cliff walls and heads directly to the viewpoint.

The trail to Diamond Creek Falls begins upstream from the parking area, where you cross Salt Creek on a small footbridge. Follow the trail to the junction and turn right. After 0.25 mile you'll pass a short trail on the left that leads to Too Much Bear Lake. From here, the trail soon joins the canyon rim where you will encounter several viewpoints with great photographic opportunities for both the canyon and falls. Rhododendrons are abundant along the trail and they begin to bloom in May and June.

At the 1.75-mile point take the steep trail that leads down 0.25 mile to a footbridge crossing Diamond Creek, through a narrow canyon, and which ends at the 100-foot Diamond Creek Falls. In contrast to the dramatic plunge of Salt Creek Falls, Diamond Creek Falls fans out over a stepped basalt face. Bluebells, salmonberry, monkeyflower, and bleeding heart all can be found along the trail.

Returning to the main trail, turn right and follow the steep switch-

Salt Creek Falls

backs to another view of Diamond Creek Falls and the trail junction to Vivian Lake. From here, you can either return by the same route you came or turn left and follow the path 1.25 miles to complete the loop, keeping an eye out for jays and chipmunk.

76

TRESTLE CREEK FALLS

Location: Umpqua National
Forest
Maps: USGS–Rose Hill, Holland
Point
Stream: Trestle Creek
Round Trip Hike Distance: 2.75
miles

Difficulty: Moderate
Height: Lower Trestle Creek Falls,
45 feet; Upper Trestle Creek Falls,
90 feet
Volume: Small
Best Season: Spring, summer, fall

SPECIAL NOTES: No fees or permits are required.

DIRECTIONS: From Cottage Grove, drive east on Row River Road
for 19.5 miles to Brice Creek Road. Turn right onto Brice Creek Road
and follow it 9 miles, passing Lund Park, to the trailhead located just past
the bridge near Champion Creek.

THE FALLS: To visit the upper falls from the trailhead, follow the path
to the right as it climbs, steeply at times, up through a series of switchbacks.
Moss-covered old-growth Douglas fir and cedar tower above the trail and
Trestle Creek canyon. After 1 mile, the trail reaches the base of the 90-
foot-high Upper Trestle Creek Falls. The falls drop from an overhanging
basalt bluff and into a moss- and fern-lined pool. The trail then passes behind the falls, and back down a narrow meandering trail for another mile
to Brice Creek. Turn left and follow the creek upstream. After 0.5 mile,

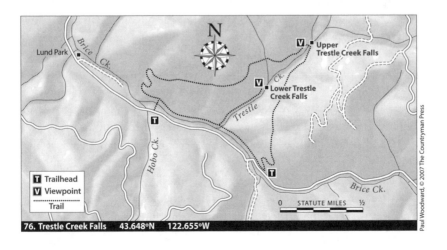

a short trail to the left leads 0.25 mile to Lower Trestle Creek Falls. To reach the parking area, continue straight for 0.25 mile.

To visit Lower Trestle Creek Falls from the trailhead, follow the path to the left downstream along Brice Creek. After 0.25 mile, turn right at the trail junction and follow it along the fern-lined creek 0.25 mile to the base of Lower Trestle Creek Falls. This 45-foot-high fan cascades down a moss-covered basalt rock face and into a small shallow pool.

This is another photographer's playground, from the old-growth cedar and fir to the moss– and fern-lined creek and the falls themselves there is no shortage of subject matter. The best light is in the early morning or late afternoon.

77

LILLIAN FALLS

Location: Waldo Lake Wilderness Area

Maps: USGS–Waldo Lake

Stream: Nettie Creek

Round Trip Hike Distance: 2.25 miles

Difficulty: Easy

Height: 80 feet

Volume: Small

Best Season: Spring, summer, fall

SPECIAL NOTES: A Northwest Forest Pass is required to park at the trailhead and is available at ranger stations and many private vendors.

DIRECTIONS: Follow Salmon Creek Road (FS 24) east from Oakridge 12.5 miles to Black Creek Road (FS 2421). Turn right onto Black Creek Road, and follow it 8 miles to its end at the Black Creek trailhead.

THE FALLS: The trail begins its climb by passing through an old clearcut before entering the Waldo Lake Wilderness Area and the lush, old-growth forest. Fir, hemlock, and cedar tower above the spring blooms of rhododendron and trillium. After 1.25 miles, just before the trail begins a steep climb, it reaches the base of the 80-foot cascade of Lillian Falls. Nettie Creek tumbles down a steep forested bluff in a series of 5- to 10-foot-high cascades, over a jumble of moss-covered boulders and downed trees.

Although Lillian Falls is not terribly impressive, it is quite scenic and there are many opportunities for the photographer. A wide-angle lens, as well as a short telephoto lens, and a polarizing filter will be useful.

78

WOLF CREEK FALLS

Location: Umpqua National Forest

Maps: USGS–Red Butte

Stream: Wolf Creek

Round Trip Hike Distance: 2.5 miles

Difficulty: Easy

Height: 30–70 feet

Volume: Small

Best Season: Spring, summer, fall, winter

SPECIAL NOTES: No fees or permits are required.

DIRECTIONS: From Roseburg take OR 138 (Diamond Lake Boulevard) west for 18 miles. Just prior to entering the small town of Glide, turn right onto Little River Road and follow it 10.5 miles to the well-marked Wolf Creek Falls trailhead.

THE FALLS: The trail begins by crossing Little River over a 150-foot-long bridge. Don't turn left, but instead follow the trail straight, to where it soon crosses Wolf Creek. The trail continues up the canyon, following the creek, while old-growth Douglas fir tower above the bigleaf maple and alder that line the stream. The trail passes by the 30-foot-high lower falls and ends a few yards later, at the base of the 70-foot-high slide of the upper falls. While the plunge of the lower falls is scenic, it's the upper falls that draws all the attention. The waterfall is a twisting slide falling over smooth basalt. During times of low flow, the water primarily flows down a well-defined chute on the right side. However, when the flow is high it fills both sides, creating a beautiful and impressive sight.

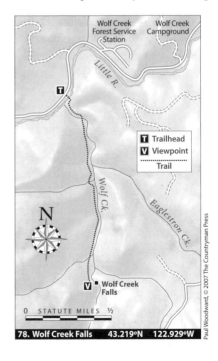

The falls is tucked away in a shallow dell, surrounded by dense vegetation, so lighting can be difficult. This is one of those waterfalls best photographed with an overcast sky. A polarizer and warming filter are extremely helpful.

79

HEMLOCK FALLS

Location: Umpqua National Forest

Maps: USGS–Quartz Mountain

Stream: Hemlock Creek

Round Trip Hike Distance: 1.25 miles

Difficulty: Moderate

Height: 80 feet

Volume: Medium

Best Season: Spring, summer, fall

SPECIAL NOTES: No fees or permits are required.

DIRECTIONS: From Roseburg, take OR 138 (Diamond Lake Boulevard) west for 18 miles. Just prior to entering the small town of Glide, turn right onto Little River Road and follow it 25.75 miles to the Lake in the Woods Campground. Park near the old ranger's cabin, and walk down the lake road a few yards to the signed trailhead.

THE FALLS: The trail descends, steeply at times, in a series of switchbacks into the small gorge which is densely forested with Douglas fir,

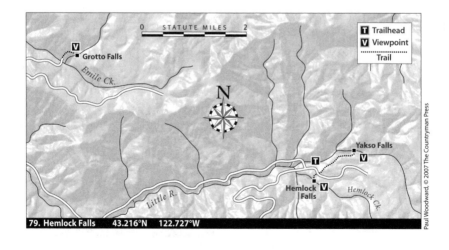

hemlock, rhododendron, and vine maple. After a little more than 0.5 mile, the trail ends at the base of 80-foot-high Hemlock Falls. Here, Hemlock Creek corkscrews down a narrow basalt gorge thickly lined with moss, and into a log-strewn pool.

The falls is nestled deep in the gorge so lighting can be difficult, but it is generally best in the afternoon hours. A warming filter and polarizer help bring out the color in the surrounding vegetation.

80

YAKSO FALLS

Location: Umpqua National
Forest
Maps: USGS–Quartz Mountain
Stream: Little River
Round Trip Hike Distance: 1.5

miles
Difficulty: Easy
Height: 70 feet
Volume: Small
Best Season: Spring, summer, fall

SPECIAL NOTES: No fees or permits are required.

DIRECTIONS: From Roseburg, take OR 138 (Diamond Lake Boulevard) west for 18 miles. Just prior to entering the small town of Glide, turn right onto Little River Road, and follow it 25.75 miles to the Lake in the Woods Campground.

THE FALLS: The trailhead is located across the road opposite the park entrance. The mostly level trail roughly parallels the river as it winds its way through Douglas fir and hemlock. The understory beneath the tall trees consists of vine maple and rhododendron, which put on a colorful show in both the spring and fall. The trail soon arrives at the pebbly beach at the base of Yakso Falls, as Little River tumbles 70 feet down into a shallow pool. The water first slides down the moss-covered rock face before being split apart by a large basalt buttress at the base. "Yakso" is the native term for hair, and it is a very fitting name for this waterfall, especially during times when the river is at low flow and the falls is more sparse.

When photographing the falls, use a slow shutter speed to emphasize its fan shape. The late afternoon light is the best when used with a polarizing filter.

81

GROTTO FALLS

Location: Umpqua National
Forest
Maps: USGS–Mace Mountain
Stream: Emile Creek
Round Trip Hike Distance: 0.75

mile
Difficulty: Easy
Height: 100 feet
Volume: Small
Best Season: Spring, summer, fall

SPECIAL NOTES: No fees or permits are required. The trail behind the falls can become very slick so use caution when hiking with small children.

DIRECTIONS: From Roseburg, take US 138 (Diamond Lake Boulevard) west for 18 miles. Just prior to entering the small town of Glide, turn right onto Little River Road, follow it 16 miles to the Coolwater Campground, and turn left onto FS 2703. Follow FS 2703 for 6.5 miles, following the Grotto Falls signs to the marked trailhead, located just past the bridge crossing Emile Creek.

THE FALLS: The trail begins by passing through an old clear-cut before making a few switchbacks up and into old-growth Douglas fir, hemlock, and rhododendron. You soon get your first view of the falls as it plunges over an undercut limestone bluff. The trail then continues behind the falls, to the trail's end on the opposite side of the falls. From here you can watch the 100-foot-high curtain of water as it crashes onto the moss-covered rocks below.

82

SUSAN CREEK FALLS

Location: Umpqua National
Forest
Maps: USGS–Old Fairview, Mace
Mountain
Stream: Susan Creek
Round Trip Hike Distance: 1.5

mile
Difficulty: Easy
Height: 50 feet
Volume: Medium
Best Season: Spring, summer, fall,
winter

SPECIAL NOTES: Located along the North Umpqua River on one of Oregon's many scenic byways, Susan Creek Falls offers a beautiful short, cool hike through old-growth Douglas fir and along rock-strewn and moss-lined Susan Creek. The trail is wheelchair accessible to the base of Susan Creek Falls. No fees or permits are required.

DIRECTIONS: From Roseburg, travel 28 miles east on OR 138. Just past milepost 28, look for the Susan Creek Falls trailhead sign, and turn left into the parking area.

THE FALLS: The milky green waters of the North Umpqua River are known to fly fishermen around the world for its summer run of steelhead trout. Some of the more famous fishermen to have tried their luck here include the prolific western writer Zane Grey and actor Clark Gable.

This well-maintained gravel trail gradually climbs through moss-covered old-growth Douglas fir, where it soon joins Susan Creek on the left. From here, the trail roughly parallels the creek until, after 0.75 mile, you reach a footbridge at the base of the falls. The falls is 50 feet high, and cascades down a moss-lined basalt cliff and into a boulder-filled plunge pool. Along the trail, look for salmonberry, iris, and rhododendron.

If you wish to follow the trail 0.5 mile further, it will bring you to the Susan Creek Indian Mounds. The now-moss-covered piles of rocks were once a spiritual site used by young natives. Here they would spend nights

Bridge below Susan Creek Falls

in a vision quest for their guardian spirit. The young boys would fast and conduct the laborious work of stacking the rocks into piles in hopes their vision would be granted.

83

FALL CREEK FALLS

Location: Umpqua National Forest

Maps: USGS–Mace Mountain

Stream: Fall Creek

Round Trip Hike Distance: 2.25 miles

Difficulty: Easy

Height: 85 feet

Volume: Small

Best Season: Spring, summer, fall, winter

SPECIAL NOTES: No fees or permits are required.

DIRECTIONS: From Roseburg, follow OR 138 east 32 miles to the signed turnoff for Fall Creek Falls on the left side of the road.

THE FALLS: The trail begins from the parking area, by crossing the alder-lined creek on a small footbridge perched above a small cascade. After a hundred yards, the trail then weaves its way through a labyrinthine crack in a huge boulder. From here, the trail roughly follows the creek through alder, moss-covered maple, towering Douglas fir, cedar, and hemlock. At just past the 0.25 mile mark, a short trail spur to the right leads up to Job's Garden, an interesting outcropping of columnar basalt. As you continue along the main trail, look for trillium and Oregon iris, which often line the trail during the spring. After 0.5 mile, you arrive at the large plunge pool at the base of Fall Creek Falls. The creek tumbles down a moss-covered basalt cliff in two tiers of 35 and 50 feet.

The area around the plunge pool offers the best opportunity for photographers. The waterfall itself is fairly open, so the midday light can create very harsh lighting conditions.

From the base of the falls, a rough trail continues up to the top of the falls and a gravel road crossing just above the waterfall. This section of the trail offers limited views of the upper section of the creek as it rushes down to the falls.

84

TOKETEE FALLS

Location: Umpqua National
Forest

Maps: USGS–Toketee Falls

Stream: North Umpqua River

Round Trip Hike Distance: 0.75
mile

Difficulty: Easy

Height: 90 feet

Volume: Large

Best Season: Spring, summer, fall,
winter

SPECIAL NOTES: This lightly used but well-maintained trail utilizes a series of stone and wooden stairs to cross a rocky outcrop and then lead down to the observation platform. They can become very slippery when wet or icy, so use caution when visiting the falls in these conditions. A Northwest Forest Pass is required to park at the trailhead and is available at ranger stations and from many private vendors.

DIRECTIONS: From Roseburg, travel east 58 miles on OR 138 to the Toketee Lake/Toketee Falls sign located just past milepost 58. Turn left onto Toketee-Rigdon Road, and follow it approximately 0.25 mile, where another sign directs you to turn left onto a short gravel road along a wooden diversion pipeline and into the parking lot and picnic area. From Diamond Lake, follow US 138 west to Toketee-Ridgon Road, turn right, and follow the signs to the parking lot.

THE FALLS: "Toketee" is the Native American word for pretty or beautiful, and it is an apt name for this secluded treasure of the cascades, which ranks as one of the most beautiful and unique waterfalls in the Northwest. Here the legendary steelhead waters of the North Umpqua River cascade 90 feet over a columnar basalt cliff formed during an early eruption of Mount Mazama, which was later transformed into nearby Crater Lake during a cataclysmic eruption.

The short trail to the falls begins at the small picnic area next to the parking lot, which is also next to the wooden 12-foot-diameter Toketee pipeline. The leaky old pipeline diverts much of the North Umpqua River to the Toketee powerhouse, located approximately 1 mile downstream. One can only imagine how the falls appeared before the river was diverted. The trail starts with a footbridge crossing a small seasonal stream, and then winds its way through 200-foot-tall Douglas fir, hemlock, and western red cedar. In the fall, vine maple adds splashes of yellow and red that are offset by the green of the conifers.

At the halfway point, the trail meets the North Umpqua River, which makes its way through a jumble of large boulders before entering the gorge that leads to the falls. From here, a few stone and wood stairs climb a small rock outcropping along the gorge, just before the trail begins its descent to the observation platform.

Toketee Falls

The platform, which is built around two Douglas firs and a yew tree, overhangs the gorge and offers a beautiful view of the falls looking down through the cedar and fir.

On the return trip, take some time to look for American dippers that frequent the water above the gorge. They are easily recognized by their upturned tail and constant "dipping" motion. In search of the aquatic insects on which they feed, these remarkable little brown birds either dive or walk directly into the swift current, and precariously walk along the bottom by grabbing firmly onto stones.

85

WATSON FALLS

Location: Umpqua National Forest

Maps: USGS–Fish Creek

Stream: Watson Creek

Round Trip Hike Distance: 0.5 mile

Difficulty: Easy

Height: 272 feet

Volume: Medium

Best Season: Spring, summer, fall

SPECIAL NOTES: A small picnic area next to the parking area and the creek make for a great family lunch spot. No fees or permits are required.

DIRECTIONS: From Roseburg, follow OR 138 east 61 miles to Fish Creek Road, just 2 miles past the Toketee Lake Road. Turn right, and after a few hundred feet turn right again into the parking area for Watson Falls.

THE FALLS: From the parking area, the top one third of the waterfall is visible. To get a better look and view the entire waterfall, cross the road to the trailhead and begin the short and moderately steep hike up to the base of the falls. The trail makes a couple of switchbacks through Douglas fir and hemlock before joining the turbulent creek. The trail soon comes to a wooden footbridge crossing the creek, as it dances under and around moss-covered boulders.

The view from the bridge offers a great photographic opportunity to capture the entire waterfall, with the creek in the foreground. The best light is in the late afternoon hours, when the sun is behind you and illuminates the entire cliff face.

After crossing the bridge, turn left, and follow the trail to its end near

Watson Falls

several very large boulders that have tumbled off the cliff. From this point you can feel the spray as the creek tumbles 272 feet off the rim of the huge rock amphitheater in a thin ribbon and hits the rocks below.

The trail makes a short loop, so on the way back you can either choose to backtrack across the bridge, or continue straight and follow the creek back to the road.

86

WHITEHORSE FALLS

Location: Umpqua National Forest

Maps: USGS–Garwood Butte

Stream: Clearwater River

Round Trip Hike Distance: At roadside

Difficulty: Easy

Height: 15 feet

Volume: Small

Best Season: Spring, fall

SPECIAL NOTES: A small observation deck overlooking the falls makes it accessible to wheelchairs. No fees or permits are required.

DIRECTIONS: From Roseburg, follow OR 138 east 63 miles to the signed turnoff for Whitehorse Falls on the left side of the road. Follow the gravel road a few hundred yards to the parking and picnic area.

THE FALLS: Old-growth Douglas fir, hemlock, and cedar surround this small punchbowl, as the Clearwater River tumbles over a small ledge and into a large plunge pool. Although much of the water is diverted for power upstream, this is still a very pretty waterfall, especially during periods of high flow. The best views of the falls are from the observation deck, but a short path leads down to the plunge pool.

Since the waterfall is in deep shade, photography can be a challenge. Use an 81A or 81B filter. Overcast days offer the best lighting conditions.

Whitehorse Falls

87

CLEARWATER FALLS

Location: Umpqua National
Forest
Maps: USGS–Diamond Lake
Stream: Clearwater River
Round Trip Hike Distance: 0.1

mile
Difficulty: Easy
Height: 35 feet
Volume: Medium
Best Season: Spring, summer, fall

SPECIAL NOTES: A small campground and picnic area make this a great family stop. No fees or permits are required.

DIRECTIONS: From Roseburg, follow OR 138 east 67 miles to the signed turnoff for Clearwater Falls Campground (8 miles past the Toketee Lake Road). Turn right onto the gravel road, and then left at the junction. Follow the road 0.5 mile to its end at the campground and picnic area.

THE FALLS: Nestled beneath old-growth Douglas fir, hemlock, and cedar, the waters of the Clearwater River tumble over, around, and under a jumbled pile of moss-covered boulders leftover from an ancient lava flow, a remnant of the region's volcanic past.

A short path leads from the parking area up to the base of the falls. It then continues upstream, to the top of the falls and a large, crystal-clear pool feeding the falls. Along the path at the top of the falls, the river has carved its way beneath the roots of the surrounding trees and under the ground. It emerges a few feet away and tumbles down the rocky falls.

Photographers will thoroughly enjoy this area, not only for the nearly limitless opportunities that the falls present, but also for the crystal-clear pool above and the rippling stream below. The best lighting conditions are typically on overcast days. A polarizer and 81A filters are a must.

Clearwater Falls

88

LEMOLO FALLS

Location: Umpqua National
Forest
Maps: USGS–Lemolo Lake
Stream: North Umpqua River
Round Trip Hike Distance: 3

miles
Difficulty: Moderate
Height: 130 feet
Volume: Large
Best Season: Spring, summer, fall

SPECIAL NOTES: No fees or permits are required.

DIRECTIONS: From Roseburg, follow OR 138 for 73 miles to FS 2610 and follow the signs toward Lemolo Lake. After 4.25 miles turn left onto the poorly marked Thorne Prairie Road and follow it 0.5 mile to Lemolo Falls Road. Turn right on Lemolo Falls Road and follow it 1.75 miles to the well-marked trailhead.

THE FALLS: At 130 feet high, Lemolo Falls is the largest waterfall on the North Umpqua River. Lemolo is the native Chinook word for "wild," and although the hydroelectric dam forming Lemolo Lake draws off much of the river's water to generate power downstream, the waterfall still maintains its wild spirit.

The trail begins at the parking area, and follows an abandoned road for 0.5 mile to an old picnic area. A few hundred yards after passing the picnic area, turn right at the trail junction and follow the path through

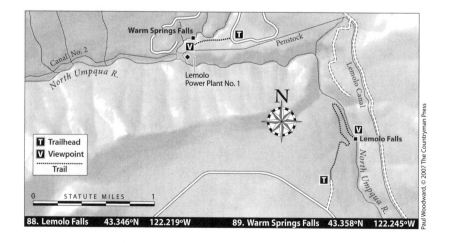

Warm Springs Falls
Canal No. 2
North Umpqua R.
Penstock
Lemolo Canal
Lemolo
Power Plant No. 1
N
Lemolo Falls
T Trailhead
V Viewpoint
Trail
North Umpqua R.
0   STATUTE MILES   1

Paul Woodward, © 2007 The Countryman Press

88. Lemolo Falls   43.346°N   122.219°W   89. Warm Springs Falls   43.358°N   122.245°W

Douglas fir, hemlock, vine maple, and rhododendron for another steep 0.75 mile to the base of the waterfall. Situated in a large basalt amphitheater, the waters of the North Umpqua River slide 130 feet down an ancient, moss-covered lava flow and into a large plunge pool.

Since the falls is located in a large amphitheater, lighting for photographing can be a challenge. Early morning or late afternoon are the best times. Use a polarizing filter to bring out the greens in the moss lining the canyon walls.

89

WARM SPRINGS FALLS

Location: Umpqua National Forest

Maps: USGS–Lemolo Lake

Stream: Warm Springs Creek

Round Trip Hike Distance: 0.5 mile

Difficulty: Easy

Height: 70 feet

Volume: Medium

Best Season: Spring, summer, fall

SPECIAL NOTES: The footing near the edge of the bluff is unstable so use caution. This trail is not recommended for small children. No fees or permits are required.

DIRECTIONS: From Roseburg, follow US 138 for 73 miles to FS 2610 and follow the signs toward Lemolo Lake. After 5.25 miles, turn left onto FS 600 and follow it 3 miles to FS 680. Turn left again onto FS 680, and follow it 1.75 miles to the Warm Springs Falls trailhead.

THE FALLS: Often overlooked for the larger Lemolo Falls, this short, lightly used 0.25-mile trail leads through Douglas fir, hemlock, and vine maple; in the spring, rhododendron, shooting stars, and trillium provide a splash of color. The trail soon breaks out onto a bluff overlooking the falls and providing a great view of Warm Springs Creek as it plunges, in a 70-foot-high curtain, into a small moss-lined pool. Like many of the falls in the area, it is framed by columnar basalt.

The best view of the falls is from the viewpoint at the trail's end. A slightly overcast day provides the best light for photographing, as do the morning and evening hours. Make sure to use a polarizing lens to bring out the greens of the moss lining the plunge pool.

90

CAMPBELL FALLS AND SOUTH UMPQUA FALLS

Location: Umpqua National
Forest
Maps: USGS–Dumont Creek,
Acker Rock
Stream: South Umpqua River
Round Trip Hike Distance: At
roadside

Difficulty: Easy
Height: Campbell Falls, 15 feet;
South Umpqua Falls, 20 feet
Volume: Large
Best Season: Spring, summer, fall,
winter

SPECIAL NOTES: No fees or permits are required. South Umpqua Falls is wheelchair accessible.

DIRECTIONS: From the Tiller Ranger Station, take County Road 46, which becomes South Umpqua Road (FS 28), for 13 miles. A small gravel pullout, located 0.75 mile past the Boulder Creek Campground, marks the viewing area. South Umpqua Falls is located 6 miles past Campbell Falls, along FS 28. Turn left into the South Umpqua group campground.

THE FALLS: I can think of very few tributes greater than having a piece of living geology named in your honor. Campbell Falls is named for Robert G. Campbell, a former US Forest Service employee, and member of this nation's greatest generation, who perished in action during World War II. Here the relatively placid waters of the South Umpqua River make a single 15-foot plunge into a turbulent pool below.

South Umpqua Falls, located just 6 miles upstream from Campbell Falls, is one of the more unique waterfalls in the region. The entire right side of the river slides gracefully down and around a large flat section of bedrock to meet the left section of the falls, which plunge 20 feet into a deep-green pool. A fish ladder, which also serves as a viewing platform, overlooks the waterfall.

The area also has historical significance to the native people of the region, who used the site as a gathering place and a communal fishery.

Several alder trees line the banks of the river, which makes this a great destination for photographing, particularly in the fall. It also means that you will not have to avoid the swimmers who are drawn to the area during the warmer summer months. The concrete fish ladder interferes with an overall view of the waterfall. However, by carefully composing the image, it can easily be excluded. The falls face west, so it's best to catch the evening light.

91

VIDAE FALLS

Location: Crater Lake National Park

Maps: USGS–Crater Lake East

Stream: Vidae Creek

Round Trip Hike Distance: At roadside

Difficulty: Easy

Height: 80 feet

Volume: Small

Best Season: Spring, summer, fall

SPECIAL NOTES: A National Park entrance pass is required and is available at the park entrance.

DIRECTIONS: From the Crater Lake Lodge, follow the Rim Drive south toward the Mazama Village. Follow the Rim Drive to the left at the park headquarters, and travel another 3 miles to a small pullout on the left, at the base of the falls.

THE FALLS: Vidae Creek cascades 80 feet down the southern slopes of Applegate Peak. At the top of the falls it makes a short, 10-foot plunge, then cascades down a cliff of loose scree. Of the three named falls inside the park boundaries, Vidae Falls is the only one that can be easily viewed or accessed.

The falls are relatively open and face southeast, and photographers will want to arrive near sunrise to capture the best light.

Vidae Falls

92

NATIONAL CREEK FALLS

Location: Rogue River National
Forest
Maps: USGS–Hamaker Butte
Stream: National Creek
Round Trip Hike Distance: 1

mile
Difficulty: Easy
Height: 80 feet
Volume: Medium
Best Season: Spring, summer, fall

SPECIAL NOTES: Located just outside the western border of Crater Lake National Park, this lightly used short walk through Douglas fir and hemlock provides relief from Crater Lake's summer crowds. No fees are required—however a small donation is recommended, and a collection box is located at the trailhead.

DIRECTIONS: From the Crater Lake Lodge, follow the Rim Drive south, toward the Mazama Village and the junction with OR 62, located just past the Annie Spring entrance station. Turn right, and follow OR 62 west 14 miles to OR 230. Turn right again, and follow OR 230 north 6 miles, where you come to a sign for National Creek Falls. Turn right onto CR 6530, and follow the signs 3.75 miles to the gravel road that leads a few hundred yards to the trailhead.

THE FALLS: The trail begins by gradually descending through a forest of large Douglas fir, hemlock, and white pine. After a short 0.25 mile, the trail makes a switchback near the top of the falls, which is obscured by a dense growth of vine maple. From here, the trail continues another 0.25 mile, through another lazy switchback, down to the base of the broad 80-foot-high cascade. Here the waters of National Creek tumble over an old basalt lava flow from ancient Mount Mazama. Near the top, a rock outcropping splits the cascade in two, before it combines again at the large splash pool.

Just downstream is an old logjam that allows you to cross to the other side of the creek and a better view of the falls from beneath several tall cedar trees.

On you return trip look for fawn lilies, Oregon iris, and vanilla leaf. The understory is primarily composed of vine maple, rhododendron, Oregon-grape, and the rhododendron-like chinkapin, with its spiny seedpods.

National Creek was a popular stop for early travelers, many of whom were on their way to test their luck in the gold fields of John Day.

National Creek Falls

93

ROGUE RIVER GORGE

Location: Rogue River National
Forest

Maps: USGS–Union Creek

Stream: Rogue River

Round Trip Hike Distance: 0.5
mile

Difficulty: Easy

Height: 30 feet

Volume: Large

Best Season: Spring, summer, fall,
winter

SPECIAL NOTES: No fees or permits are required.

DIRECTIONS: From Diamond Lake, follow US 138 to the junction with US 230. Turn right onto US 230, and follow it 24 miles to the Rogue River Gorge viewpoint on the right.

THE FALLS: The short, paved interpretive trail starts at the parking area and leads 100 yards to the rim of the gorge. The fenced trail follows the rim of the deep, narrow, moss-lined gorge, which is actually an ancient lava tube, upstream for 0.25 mile. Several observation decks along

Rogue River Gorge

the way allow spectacular views of the churning Rogue River below. Just before the trail begins to loop back to the parking area, a viewpoint overlooks the river as it tumbles 30 feet into the gorge.

This area is a photographer's playground, so plan on spending a few hours. The best light is in the late afternoon or evening. A polarizing and graduated neutral density filter are very useful.

94

MILL CREEK FALLS AND BARR CREEK FALLS

Location: Rogue River National Forest
Maps: USGS–Prospect South
Stream: Mill Creek, Barr Creek
Round Trip Hike Distance: 1 mile

Difficulty: Easy
Height: Mill Creek Falls, 173 feet; Barr Creek Falls, 180 feet
Volume: Mill Creek Falls, large; Barr Creek falls, medium
Best Season: Spring, fall, winter

SPECIAL NOTES: No fees or permits are required. Use caution when hiking next to the canyon rim.

DIRECTIONS: From the town of Prospect, drive west on US 42 to Mill Creek Road and turn left. Follow Mill Creek Road for 0.25 mile, then veer left and follow the road for another 0.75 mile to the Mill Creek Falls parking area.

THE FALLS: The trail begins at the parking area, and heads through second-growth Douglas fir and hemlock on its way to the rim of the Rogue River Canyon. The trail is part of the Mill Creek Botanical Trail. Mill Creek Falls Scenic Area is owned by the Boise Cascade Corporation, and they maintain this recreational trail, which leads to the falls. Along the way, a series of markers name and describe many of the plants along the path. After 0.25 mile the trail nears the canyon rim, and forks. Turn left, and after a few hundred yards you reach the cliff-top viewpoint, which looks across the canyon to the very impressive Mill Creek Falls as it hurtles off a basalt cliff and plunges 173 feet to the rocks and Rogue River below.

To reach Barr Creek Falls, turn right at the trail junction and follow the short trail spur to a viewpoint perched on a rock outcropping on the edge of the canyon rim. Barr Creek tumbles down the opposite side of the canyon wall 180 feet, onto moss-covered rock along the Rogue River. The falls actually consist of two widely spaced segments, but during the summer months the left segment is often reduced to little more than a trickle.

Both Mill Creek Falls and Barr Creek Falls tumble into a spectacular deep, narrow, boulder-strewn section of the Rogue River Gorge known as the "Avenue of the Giant Boulders." This section of the Rogue River is a favorite playground for whitewater kayakers around the nation.

Since you are shooting across the canyon, photographers will want to bring a small telephoto lens (100mm). A polarizer and UV filter may also be of use.

95

RED BLANKET FALLS AND STUART FALLS

Location: Sky Lakes Wilderness Area

Maps: USGS–Union Creek

Stream: Red Blanket Creek

Round Trip Hike Distance: Red Blanket Falls, 6 miles; Stuart Falls,

8.5 miles

Difficulty: Moderate to difficult

Height: Red Blanket Falls, 60 feet; Stuart Falls, 40 feet

Volume: Medium

Best Season: Spring, summer, fall

SPECIAL NOTES: A Northwest Forest Pass is required to park at the trailhead, and is available at ranger stations and many private vendors.

DIRECTIONS: From the small town of Prospect, follow Butte Falls Road for 1 mile to Red Blanket Road. Turn left onto Red Blanket Road, follow it 0.5 mile, and veer right onto gravel FS 6205. Follow FS 6205 for 12 miles to its end at the trailhead.

THE FALLS: From the parking area, the trail sets out through a Douglas fir and hemlock grove. After passing the Crater Lake National Park boundary marker, you officially enter the Sky Lakes Wilderness Area. The trail continues up along the rim of the canyon, with glimpses of the creek through the Douglas fir and hemlock, while beneath the tall trees grow smaller dogwood trees, rhododendron, and the holly-like Oregon-grape.

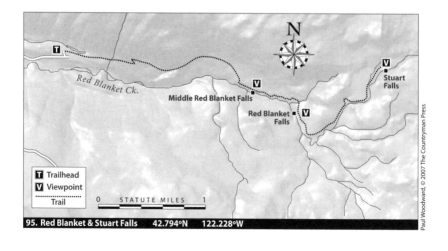

T Trailhead
V Viewpoint
········· Trail

Red Blanket Ck.

Middle Red Blanket Falls

Red Blanket Falls

Stuart Falls

0 STATUTE MILES 1

95. Red Blanket & Stuart Falls   42.794°N   122.228°W

Paul Woodward, © 2007 The Countryman Press

After 2.5 miles, the trail passes two small 20- to 25-foot-high cascades, often referred to as Middle Red Blanket Falls. Continuing along for another 0.5 mile brings you to the base of Red Blanket Falls. The creek first drops 10 feet, just before it tumbles another 50 feet down a jagged basalt bluff and into a small but deep pool. During times of normal flow, the main center chute is often framed by smaller rivulets on either side.

The falls is named for the creek, which got its name from early settlers who used to purchase handcrafted red blankets from the native Takelma people living nearby.

At the junction stay to the left, following the trail it as it climbs along the creek. In addition to the fir and hemlock, lodgepole pine begin to make an appearance, as do huckleberries, which in late summer are perfect for a trailside snack. Stay left at the second junction, and after another 0.5 mile you arrive at the base of the 40-foot-high fan of Stuart Falls as it cascades down a moss-covered outcrop of columnar basalt.

96

ROUGH RIDER FALLS

Location: Rogue River National
Forest

Maps: USGS–Hamaker Butte

Stream: Rogue River

Round Trip Hike Distance: 9.5
miles

Difficulty: Difficult

Height: 50 feet

Volume: Medium

Best Season: Spring, summer, fall

SPECIAL NOTES: No fees or permits are required.

DIRECTIONS: From Diamond Lake, follow US 138 to the junction with US 230. Turn right onto US 230, and follow it 5 miles to the Crater Rim Viewpoint.

THE FALLS: The trail begins by gradually descending through a relatively open forest of Douglas fir, hemlock, and lodgepole pine. After 0.5 mile the trail reaches the rim of the canyon and forks; turn right and follow the trail downstream. From here the trail follows the rim of the canyon carved by the river from a deep layer of ash that was deposited during the eruption of Mount Mazama, which created Crater Lake 7,700 years ago. The trail provides views of the Rogue River's sometimes placid, sometimes churning, crystal-clear water below. After 4.25 miles you hear the roar of the falls and the trail makes a switchback down into the canyon. On the left, a rough trail spur leads to the river and the base of the falls. The Rogue River drops 50 turbulent feet onto a jumble of moss-covered rocks and logs. This is a very scenic falls, and an equally scenic trail.

Photographers will want to visit on an overcast day, since lighting on a sunny day can be extremely difficult. A polarizer and warming filter are useful tools to have in the camera bag.

IV. Eastern Oregon and Eastern Washington

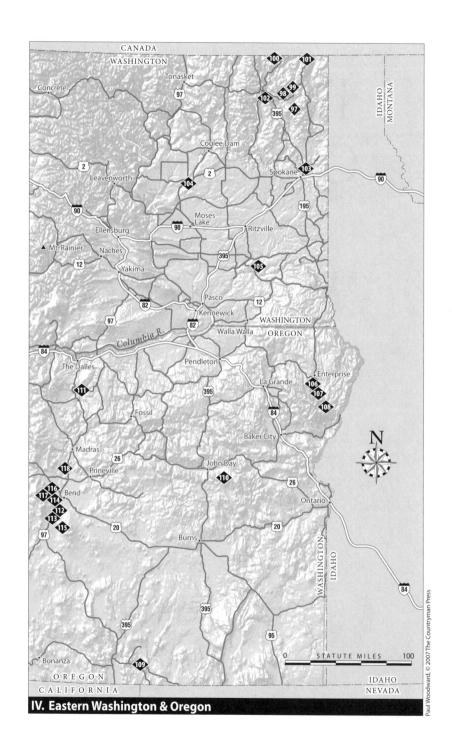

IV. Eastern Washington & Oregon

INTRODUCTION

The northeast corner of Washington is also known as the Okanogan Highlands, and includes the cities of Colville and Spokane. It is characterized by rounded mountains (as high as 8,000 feet) and deep, narrow valleys. Spokane, with a population of 200,000, is the largest city in the region and has a very active arts and cultural establishment.

To the south are the rolling farmlands of the Palouse. During the spring the fields are awash with a geometric quilt of green wheat sprouts, red clover, and the bright yellow flowers of canola. This seasonal display brings tourists and photographers from around the region. The most popular vista is Steptoe Butte, located just north of Colfax. The 3,612-foot-high quartzite bluff offers a birds-eye view of the colorful display below.

Tucked away in the northeastern corner of Oregon is perhaps the region's most spectacular scenery. Along the border with Idaho lies Hells Canyon, the deepest canyon in North America. You can't help but feel exceptionally small as you stand on the edge and look across the endless ridges. Just a few miles to the south of Hells Canyon lie the Wallowa Mountains. Nicknamed the "Alps of Oregon," the Wallowas are much more aligned with the Rockies than the volcanic peaks of the Cascades. The granite and marble peaks of the Wallowas reach a height of nearly 10,000 feet, and contain more than 500 miles of hiking trails. They are also home to the 385,541-acre Eagle Cap Wilderness Area—Oregon's largest.

In the southeastern portion of Oregon are the northern reaches of the Great Basin. With regards to climate and geology, this region of the Pacific Northwest is much more closely aligned with Nevada, Utah, and Wyoming. Broad, wide basins—with an average elevation above 4,000 feet—separate fault-block mountains which, like Steens Mountain, can reach a height of nearly 10,000 feet. Southeastern Oregon is also the least populated region in the northwest, with a population density of less than one person per square mile—comparable to that of Alaska.

Climate

The climate east of the Cascades is extremely varied. The northeastern corner of Washington has a climate similar to that of the Rocky Mountains, while in the southeast portion of Oregon conditions are very dry, with a climate much like that of the Great Basin.

The northeastern corner of Washington, near Colville and Spokane and the high Columbia Plateau—which covers much of eastern and central Washington as well as portions of north-central Oregon—is a land of extremes. Annual rainfall varies from less than 10 inches in the drier valleys of the Palouse to as much as 60 inches in the Wallowa Mountains, with the majority occurring in winter. Winter temperatures can hover near or below freezing for weeks, while in the summer temperatures can easily reach well above 100 degrees. The region has recorded both the highest and lowest temperatures in the region: 119 degrees in Pendleton, Oregon; and -54 degrees in Seneca, Oregon.

The climate of the southeast portion of Oregon is the driest in the Northwest. Many places experience an annual rainfall of less than 10 inches, with the majority occurring in winter as snowfall. The Alvord Desert, a dry alkali playa located on the east side of Steens Mountain, typically sees less than 5 inches a year. Like the Columbia Plateau to the north, winter temperatures can hover near or below freezing for weeks, while summer temperatures can reach well above 100 degrees. Not only is this a land of extreme seasonal temperature ranges, but daily temperatures can vary from near freezing at night to near 90 degrees in the afternoon.

Precautions

Many of the trails in this book pass by steep cliffs and rushing whitewater, and in many instances the edge can be unstable and/or slippery. Stay on the trails in these areas and refrain from climbing over fences and railings.

When traveling in the desert regions, even if you are planning on taking only short hikes, it is always extremely important to carry extra water. A good rule of thumb is to triple the amount of water you would normally carry. Be sure to use proper sunscreen, and remember to take your time.

In the Palouse region of Washington and the southeastern portion of Oregon, the availability of gasoline can be a real concern. It is not uncommon to make a round trip of over 200 miles without encountering a single service station. If you are planning on a long trip, make sure your tank is full and consider carrying extra fuel.

Much of eastern Washington and Oregon are classified as open range. Use caution when you see the yellow OPEN RANGE or LIVESTOCK warning signs. Be aware that if you are involved in an accident, not only will you be responsible for the repairs to your car, but you are also liable for any resulting injury to or death of the livestock.

Attractions

• In 1941, the Grand Coulee Dam was built on the Columbia River as part of The Columbia River Basin Project. The dam is the largest concrete structure in the United States, containing 12 million cubic yards of concrete. The dam backs up the Columbia River, creating 130-mile-long Lake Roosevelt, which is named for President Franklin D. Roosevelt. In addition to the dam, Lake Roosevelt National Recreation Area is home to both historic Fort Spokane and St. Paul's Mission.

- The Whitman Mission National Historic Site is located 8 miles west of Walla Walla and documents the 1847 Whitman "Massacre" of Marcus and Narcissa Whitman along with 12 other settlers by the Cayuse tribe, which lived near the mission. The memorial documents the events leading up to the massacre, the massacre itself, and the controversial aftermath, as well as exploring the reasons for this tragic clash of cultures.

- Traveling 24 miles north of Imnaha, along a steep, winding gravel road, brings you to the awe-inspiring Hat Point Overlook. At an elevation of 6,982 feet, the overlook is perched on the western edge of Hells Canyon, and overlooks the deepest gorge in North America. The thin ribbon of the Snake River winds its way through the canyon, more than 5,700 feet below, with Idaho's 9,000-foot-tall Seven Devils Mountains visible in the distance.

- The John Day Fossil Beds National Monument is divided into three units: the Painted Hills Unit, northwest of Mitchell; the Clarno Unit, 20 miles west of Fossil; and the Sheep Rock Unit, located northwest of Dayville. The Sheep Rock Unit is also the location of the visitor center, which is open daily from March through October. The center has wonderful displays of the fossils discovered in the monument. Congress established the John Day Fossil Beds National Monument in 1975, and its three units encompass a total of 14,000 acres. Each of the units offer short interpretive trails that explore the sedimentary rocks preserving a 40-million-year record of plant and animal life during the Cenozoic Era (the "Age of Mammals and Flowering Plants").

- The Malheur National Wildlife Refuge headquarters is located 37 miles south of Burns, and is one of Oregon's true wonders. The refuge manages over 187,000 acres of wetlands, riparian areas, meadows, and sagebrush and juniper uplands. Over 320 species of birds, 58 species of mammals, and 10 species of native fish can be found on the refuge during the year. Over 130 species of birds nest on the refuge. Sandhill cranes, egrets, heron, ibis, pelicans, avocets, coots, grebes, swans, and numerous ducks and songbirds are common sights within the refuge, as are mule deer and pronghorn antelope.

97

CRYSTAL FALLS

Location: Little Pend Oreille National Wildlife Refuge

Maps: USGS–Park Rapids

Stream: Little Pend Oreille River

Round Trip Hike Distance: At roadside

Difficulty: Easy

Height: 50 feet

Volume: Medium

Best Season: Spring, summer, fall

SPECIAL NOTES: No fees or access permits are required.

DIRECTIONS: From Colville, follow OR 20 east for 14 miles to the signed pullout for Crystal Falls.

THE FALLS: A viewing area located next to the pullout offers a nice view of the falls. The Little Pend Oreille River flows through ponderosa pine, montane firs, and sagebrush as it cascades down a rock-strewn creek-bed, before plunging the final 10 feet into a shallow rocky pool. The nearby refuge offers the opportunity to observe a diverse population of wildlife. Over 180 species of birds call the refuge home for at least part of the year. It is also one of the few places in the state where moose roam freely.

The falls face southwest, and the best light to photograph occurs in late afternoon.

98

DOUGLAS FALLS

Location: Douglas Falls Grange Park

Maps: USGS–Colville

Stream: Mill Creek

Round Trip Hike Distance: At roadside

Difficulty: Easy

Height: 60 feet

Volume: Medium

Best Season: Spring, summer, fall, winter

SPECIAL NOTES: No fees or access permits are required. The falls is wheelchair accessible.

DIRECTIONS: Driving east from Colville on OR 20 for 1.25 miles, turn left onto Aladdin Road. Follow Aladdin Road for 2 miles, and turn left onto Douglas Road. Follow Douglas Road another 3 miles to the entrance of Douglas Falls Grange Park.

THE FALLS: The railed viewpoint for the falls is located next to the parking area for the picnic grounds. This 60-foot-high falls is a classic fan, sliding down a rounded basalt rock face and into a shallow pool. The waterfall is named for R. H. Douglas, who built a gristmill on the site, which was later converted into a lumber mill to supply wood to nearby Fort Colville.

The waterfall is totally exposed, so the best light for photography occurs near sunrise, sunset, or on an overcast day.

99

MARBLE CREEK FALLS

Location: Colville National Forest
Maps: USGS–Gillette Mountain
Stream: Marble Creek
Round Trip Hike Distance: 0.25 mile

Difficulty: Easy
Height: 30 feet
Volume: Small
Best Season: Spring, fall

SPECIAL NOTES: No fees or access permits are required.

DIRECTIONS: From Colville, follow OR 20 east 1.25 miles to CR 700 and turn left. Follow this road for 2 miles to Aladdin Road, and turn right. Travel along Aladdin Road for 11 miles to FS 200, on the left. Pull onto FS 200, and park along the side of the road.

THE FALLS: From the informal parking area, follow the road (which quickly becomes an overgrown path) as it follows alongside Marble Creek for a few hundred yards to an overgrown viewpoint looking

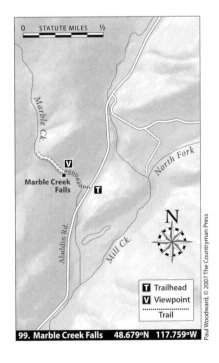
99. Marble Creek Falls   48.679°N   117.759°W

down onto the waterfall. Marble Creek plunges 30 feet down a sheer rock face and into a small, turbulent pool. Although small in stature, this waterfall, surrounded by fir and alder, can be quite scenic in the early morning and late evening light.

100

SHEEP CREEK FALLS

Location: Colville National Forest **Difficulty:** Moderate
Maps: USGS–Northport **Height:** 120 feet
Stream: Big Sheep Creek **Volume:** Large
Round Trip Hike Distance: 3 **Best Season:** Spring, summer, fall
miles

SPECIAL NOTES: No fees or access permits are required.

DIRECTIONS: Follow OR 25 from Northport north, crossing the Columbia River, 0.5 mile to CR 4220. Turn left and follow CR 4220 another 0.5 mile to the unmarked dirt road on the left, and park at one of the several pullouts.

THE FALLS: From the parking area, follow the road for a little less than 1 mile to the rim of the canyon carved by Big Sheep Creek. Turn left, and follow the well-worn trail another 0.5 mile upstream to the several viewpoints, both overlooking the falls and at its base. Big Sheep Creek roars 120 feet down a cleft in the basalt cliff, and into a deep pool.

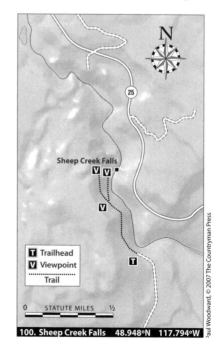

Sheep Creek Falls

T Trailhead
V Viewpoint
········· Trail

0   STATUTE MILES   ½

100. Sheep Creek Falls   48.948°N   117.794°W

Paul Woodward, © 2007 The Countryman Press

101

PEWEE FALLS

Location: Colville National Forest

Maps: USGS–Boundary Dam

Stream: Pewee Creek

Round Trip Hike Distance: 2 miles; boat access, 3 miles

Difficulty: Easy to moderate

Height: 200 feet

Volume: Medium

Best Season: Spring, summer, fall, winter

SPECIAL NOTES: No fees or access permits are required.

DIRECTIONS: From Metaline Falls, travel south on OR 31 for 1 mile, and turn right onto Crawford Park Road. Follow Crawford Park Road another 11 miles, to the boat launch just above the Boundary Dam.

THE FALLS: The waterfall is located approximately 2 miles by boat up the inlet for Pewee Creek. By far the easiest route to view the falls is by boat. It is also the most spectacular, as Pewee Creek plunges 200 feet down a barren rock face, directly into the Boundary Dam Reservoir.

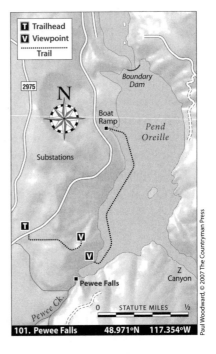

A land-based view is also possible for the more adventurous hiker. Follow Crawford Park Road for 1.25 miles back toward the intersection with OR 31, to an unmarked parking area on the left side of the road. From here, a very rough 0.25-mile-long trail leads along the power lines, and then up a small hill with a view looking down onto the falls.

102

MEYERS FALLS

Location: Kettle Falls
Maps: USGS–Kettle Falls
Stream: Colville River
Round Trip Hike Distance: At roadside

Difficulty: Easy
Height: 85 feet
Volume: Large
Best Season: Spring, summer, fall

SPECIAL NOTES: No fees or access permits are required. The access road is on private property and not open to the public or auto traffic.

DIRECTIONS: From Kettle Falls, travel 0.5 mile south on Meyers Road to the power station just below Meyers Reservoir. Turn right on the unmarked dirt road and follow it another 0.5 mile to an unmarked pullout near the road's end.

THE FALLS: From the parking area, walk a few feet to the edge of the river. The Colville River tumbles 85 feet over a basalt rock outcropping, next to a small power station operated by the Washington Water Power Company. Although some of the water from the Colville River is diverted to generate power, the waterfall is still impressive. The falls is named for an early pioneer to the area.

103

SPOKANE FALLS

Location: Spokane
Maps: USGS–Spokane NW
Stream: Spokane River
Round Trip Hike Distance: At roadside

Difficulty: Easy
Height: 80 feet
Volume: Large
Best Season: Spring, summer, fall, winter

SPECIAL NOTES: No fees or permits are required. The falls is wheelchair accessible.

DIRECTIONS: Spokane Falls is located along the Riverfront Park in downtown Spokane. From I-90, take the Division Street exit and follow it north to Spokane Falls Boulevard. Turn left, and follow the boulevard to the entrance of Riverfront Park.

THE FALLS: Although the waterfall has undergone tremendous development and a large amount of the river is diverted to generate power, it still remains an impressive sight. The Spokane River is split in two by Canada Island, a large basalt outcrop. On either side, the river cascades through a series of channels cut by it into the basalt riverbed. Several hundred yards downstream, below the hydroelectric dam, the river again drops down a series of basalt chutes.

In 1974, Spokane played host to the World's Fair, which was primarily located at Riverfront Park. Consequently, the falls were a major attraction. A tram was even built to give visitors an up-close view. If you choose not to take the tram, there are great views of the falls available from the walkway along the park and the bridge crossing the river to Canada Island.

104

DRY FALLS

Location: Sun Lakes State Park
Maps: USGS–Coulee City
Stream: Missoula Floodwaters
Round Trip Hike Distance: At roadside

Difficulty: Easy
Height: 400 feet
Volume: Large
Best Season: Spring, summer, fall, winter

SPECIAL NOTES: No fees or access permits are required for the overlook. A day-use fee is required for Sun Lakes Park. The viewpoint overlooking Dry Falls is wheelchair accessible.

DIRECTIONS: Travel north from Ephrata on OR 283 to Soap Lake. In Soap Lake, turn north onto OR 17, and follow it 17 miles to Sun Lakes State Park.

THE FALLS: True to its name, water no longer flows over the falls. However, 10,000 years ago this was the site of the largest waterfall the planet has ever seen. At 400 feet high and over 3.5 miles wide, it was more than 10 times the size of the present-day Niagara Falls (165 feet high and 1 mile wide). The source of this water was Glacier Lake Mis-

Dry Falls

soula, an enormous lake covering more than 300,000 square miles of northwest Montana formed when Ice Age glaciers dammed the Clark Fork River. As the lake grew larger, so did the pressure on the ice dam until it could no longer hold, releasing a volume of water comparable to that of Lake Ontario and a flow estimated to be greater than all the rivers of the world combined over the Idaho Panhandle, eastern Washington, and the northern Oregon landscape.

As the torrent of floodwaters approached the area, it was more than 300 feet deep and racing along at 65 miles per hour. The original cliff creating the falls was located near the town of Soap Lake, but these tremendous hydraulic forces gradually ate away at the cliff, and the falls retreated 17 miles to its present location—a process known as "headward erosion."

Remarkably, this was not a single isolated event, but may have occurred as many as 100 times, at intervals of between 50 to 100 years. These floods, now known as the Missoula Floods, are responsible for much of the geology of eastern Washington and the Columbia River Gorge. Grand Coulee, the Channeled Scablands, and Palouse Falls in Washington, and the hanging valleys creating the waterfalls in the Columbia River Gorge, can all trace their origins to this incredible geological event.

It should be noted that prior to the turn of the century, the geology of eastern Washington was not fully understood. In the 1920s, a single geologist, J Harlen Bretz, first proposed the idea of the Missoula Floods and was soundly criticized for his ideas. Undeterred, Bretz continued his research and compiled a mountain of evidence supporting his flooding theory. Finally, after more than 40 years, his evidence (combined with modern geologic methods), was accepted, and the Missoula Floods are now widely believed to be the single most dominant event in shaping the eastern Washington landscape.

The Dry Falls overlook, located 1.5 miles past the entrance to Sun Lakes State Park, provides the best view of the ancient falls and plunge pool. A trail from the overlook leads down to the base of the cliffs, where it connects to a small network of trails that explore the many small lakes that now occupy the old floodplain. To explore the plunge pool by car, travel back to the park, where a park road makes a short loop through the area. Sagebrush and rabbit brush dominate the landscape; however, in spring the sunflower-like balsamroot, purple lupines, bluebells, penstemon, and phlox all bring a splash of color to the otherwise dry desert.

Sunrise and sunset provide the best light for photographing this wide-open landscape. For photographing Dry Falls, a wide-angle lens is essential. A polarizing filter and graduated neutral density filter are also useful.

105

PALOUSE FALLS

Location: Palouse Falls State Park
Maps: USGS–Palouse Falls
Stream: Palouse River
Round Trip Hike Distance: At roadside

Difficulty: Easy
Height: 198 feet
Volume: Large
Best Season: Spring, summer, fall, winter

SPECIAL NOTES: A Washington Parks day-use fee is required, and is available at the park entrance. This is definitely rattlesnake country! Avoid stepping over, or reaching around, rocks and brush without checking carefully first.

The viewpoint and 0.25-mile long trail along the rim of the gorge is wheelchair accessible.

DIRECTIONS: From Washtucna, drive 6 miles south on OR 260 to the junction with OR 261. Turn left onto OR 261 and follow it 8.75 miles to the gravel Palouse Falls Road. Turn left, following the park signs, and drive 2.5 miles to Palouse Falls State Park.

THE FALLS: Palouse Falls is another one of the spectacular natural features of Washington State. Surrounded by the rolling farmlands of the Palouse countryside, the Palouse River plunges into a huge, deep-green pool located at the bottom of a gorge carved by glacial floods 10,000 years ago.

The viewpoints along the rim are a long way from the waterfall itself; however, they do provide an excellent view of the falls and the gorge that is an integral part of the experience. A rough maze of trails does lead upstream and offer a closer view; however, the state has posted no trespassing signs halfway up the trails.

The gorge, which the river has carved itself into, is composed of layers of ancient columnar basalt, the remnants of the repeated lava flows that covered the area hundreds of thousands of years ago. Near the lip of the falls, several basalt spires overlook the river.

In spring, wildflowers such as balsamroot, lupine, and wild hyacinth bloom along the cliffs of the gorge, bringing color to the surrounding desert landscape. Additional color is provided by a rainbow that frequently forms in the clouds of mist, near the base of the falls.

For close-ups of the falls, photographers will want to bring a moderate telephoto lens. A polarizing filter will also help bring out the colors of the rainbow that forms at the base of the falls.

106

FALLS CREEK FALLS

Location: Eagle Cap Wilderness Area

Maps: USGS–Chief Joseph Mountain

Stream: Falls Creek

Round Trip Hike Distance: 0.5 mile

Difficulty: Easy

Height: 90 feet

Volume: Small

Best Season: Spring, summer, fall

SPECIAL NOTES: A Northwest Forest Pass is required to park at the trailhead and is available at ranger stations and from many private vendors.

DIRECTIONS: From La Grande, follow US 82 north 65 miles to Enterprise. Turn right onto Hurricane Creek Road and continue on it for 9 miles, following the Hurricane Creek signs to the road's end at the trailhead parking area.

THE FALLS: The trail begins on the south end of the parking area opposite of the horse loading area, and passes through a small grove of aspen and lodgepole pine. Just a hundred yards from the trailhead, the trail arrives at the junction with the LeGore Lake Trail. Follow the trail to the right (LeGore Lake Trail) as it leads a short 0.25 mile to the edge of Falls Creek, and a great view of Falls Creek Falls just upstream. The falls tumbles 90 feet over the barren granite face, which has been scoured clean by repeated spring floods and winter avalanches. Snowcapped Sawtooth Peak and Twin Peak are high off in the distance.

Since the falls and creek are fully exposed, the best light is early in the morning near sunrise. While the falls is not exceptionally photogenic, the surrounding area is, and it is well worth a little extra effort to hike farther up Hurricane Creek and explore the area.

107

BC CREEK FALLS

Location: Wallowa Lake State Park
Maps: USGS–Wallowa Mountains
Stream: BC Creek
Round Trip Hike Distance: 2.75 miles
Difficulty: Easy
Height: 80 feet
Volume: Small
Best Season: Spring, summer, fall

SPECIAL NOTES: No permits or access fees are required. Due to its proximity to the resort and campground, the trail can become crowded during the spring and summer. There are several steep drop-offs along the trail, and care should be taken when hiking with small children.

DIRECTIONS: From La Grande, follow US 82 for 75 miles, through Enterprise, to Joseph. From Joseph, follow the state park signs another 6 miles, along the east shore of Wallowa Lake. Pass by the tramway station and continue 0.25 mile to the road's end. The Wallowa Lake trailhead is located on the left, next to the power station.

THE FALLS: The trail begins by passing behind the small power plant

BC Creek Falls

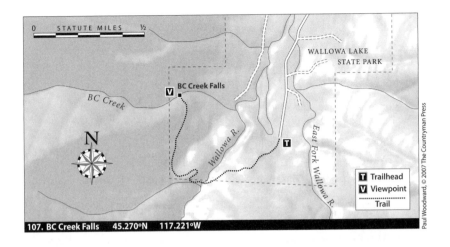

107. BC Creek Falls   45.270°N   117.221°W

Paul Woodward, © 2007 The Countryman Press

located at the end of the road. Stay to the right as the trail climbs over and around moss-covered rocks, and through fir and aspen. After 0.25 mile, the trail forks; stay to the right and follow the Chief Joseph Trail, where you will soon join the 100-foot-deep gorge as the West Fork of the Wallowa River cuts its way to the lake. A short trail spur to the right leads a few hundred yards down to a rock outcrop that offers a wonderful view of the river as it flows through the gorge.

Continuing along the main trail another 0.25 mile brings you to a footbridge, crossing the clear and very cold waters of the river. From here, the trail begins a series of switchbacks up a small boulder field, offering views of the river below. The trail gradually levels off, and soon you come to a cliffside viewpoint overlooking the south end of Wallowa Lake, and the campground and resort with Mount Howard and its tram above. From here it's only another 0.25 mile to the bridge that crosses between the upper and lower tiers of the BC Creek Falls. The waterfall is composed of two 40-foot-high fans, with only the upper tier visible.

108

IMNAHA FALLS

Location: Eagle Cap Wilderness
Area
Maps: USGS–Deadman Point
Stream: Imnaha River
Round Trip Hike Distance: 11.5

miles
Difficulty: Difficult
Height: 15 feet
Volume: Large
Best Season: Spring, summer, fall

SPECIAL NOTES: A day-use parking fee is required at the trailhead.

DIRECTIONS: Drive 8 miles east from Joseph on Imnaha Road, to Wallowa Mountain Road, and turn right. Follow the road 32 miles to CR 3960 and turn right. Follow CR 3960 for another 9 miles to Indian Crossing Campground.

THE FALLS: From the campground, the trail follows the river as it passes through a sparse forest of lodgepole pine and Douglas fir. After 2 miles, a short trail spur on the left leads a few hundred yards to the Blue Hole. Here the Imnaha River squeezes through a narrow gorge, and then opens to a spectacular deep-blue pool. Continuing along the main trail, look for fireweed, balsamroot, and yarrow lining the path. Another 3.25 miles brings you to another left-hand trail spur. This spur leads to Cataract Gorge, where the river boils through a narrow slot in the in the bedrock. From here, it is just 0.5 mile along the main trail to Imnaha Falls. The

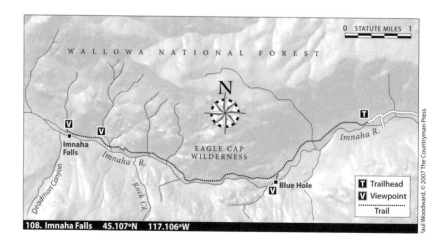

falls is a 15-foot plunge into a deep-blue pool, as the river is squeezed from a narrow rock chute.

109

DEEP CREEK FALLS

Location: Adel
Maps: USGS–Adel
Stream: Deep Creek
Round Trip Hike Distance: At roadside

Difficulty: Easy
Height: 30 feet
Volume: Large
Best Season: Spring, fall, winter

SPECIAL NOTES: No fees or access permits are required. Use caution when entering and exiting the small gravel roadside pullout.

DIRECTIONS: From Lakeview, follow US 140 east 30 miles, toward the small town of Adel. If you are coming from Adel, the falls is located just 2.75 miles west along US 140.

THE FALLS: This scenic little waterfall is located in Deep Creek Canyon, and is in the heart of the Oregon outback. Here Deep Creek drops 30 feet, in a segmented falls which is framed by columnar basalt. Sagebrush and a few juniper trees line the creek. Perhaps the most scenic time to visit the waterfall is in the winter, when it begins to freeze and the spray coats the basalt with ice.

The best view of the falls is from the shoulder of the road, so photographers should consider bringing a short telephoto lens and polarizer.

110

STRAWBERRY FALLS

Location: Strawberry Mountain
Wilderness Area
Maps: USGS–Strawberry Mountain
Stream: Strawberry Creek
Round Trip Hike Distance: 6
miles
Difficulty: Moderate
Height: 80 feet
Volume: Small
Best Season: Spring, summer, fall

SPECIAL NOTES: No fees or access permits are required.

DIRECTIONS: From John Day, follow US 26 east 13 miles to Prairie City. In Prairie City, turn right on Bridge Street and follow it 11 miles to its end at the Strawberry Campground.

THE FALLS: The trail begins at the map board in Strawberry Campground, and from here it climbs through a forest of white fir, Oregon-grape, and huckleberries. Stay to the right at the fork 1 mile from the trailhead, as the trail then crosses a jumble of moss-covered boulders—a remnant of a large Ice Age landslide. During

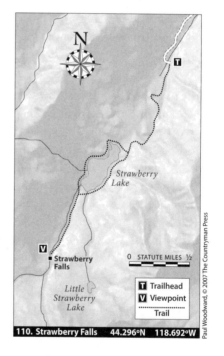

110. Strawberry Falls   44.296°N   118.692°W

the summer, the sounds of the creek can be heard from the trail but not seen, since its water flows beneath the landslide. After traveling another 0.25 mile, turn right and follow the trail another few hundred yards to the shores of Strawberry Lake.

The trail encircles the lake, so either direction will bring you to the trail junction leading to the falls on the far side of the lake. The left route is approximately 0.5 mile shorter, but the trail to the right is more scenic, providing a view of the rugged mountain cliff overlooking the lake.

Strawberry Falls

At the far end of the lake, follow the trail as it makes a moderately steep climb for another mile along Strawberry Creek. At the switchback leading to the left, a very short trail spur to the right leads to the base of Strawberry Falls. The falls is a broad horsetail, cascading down a moss-covered basalt rock face and onto the jumble of rocks below.

The Strawberry Mountain Wilderness Area has an extremely diverse eco-logical makeup. Jutting up more than 9,000 feet from the surrounding prairie and sagebrush desert, this glacier-carved alpine oasis sustains a healthy pop-ulation of native Rocky Mountain elk, as well as deer, antelope, black bear, cougar, bighorn sheep, grouse, bald eagles, pine marten, and beaver. In all, more than 370 birds and mammals call the wilderness home.

WHITE RIVER FALLS

Location: White River Falls State Park

Maps: USGS–Maupin

Stream: White River

Round Trip Hike Distance: 0.75 mile

Difficulty: Easy

Height: 130 feet

Volume: Large

Best Season: Spring, summer, fall, winter

SPECIAL NOTES: No permits or access fees are required. There are sev-eral steep drop-offs along the trail, and care should be taken when hik-ing with small children. The viewpoint overlooking the upper tier of the falls is wheelchair accessible.

DIRECTIONS: From Maupin, follow US 197 north for 9 miles to the intersection with OR 216. Turn right onto OR 216, and follow it 4 miles to the entrance to the White River Falls State Park on the right.

THE FALLS: From the parking area, a short trail leads to a viewpoint overlooking the 90-foot-high segmented waterfall as it plunges over a basalt shelf and into a turbulent pool below. The White River then churns through a narrow chute before dumping into a large pool, just above the 40-foot-high second tier. Due to the distance between the upper and lower tiers, the lower tier is often (and perhaps more accurately) called Middle White River Falls.

To get a better view of the falls, follow the path to the left that leads 0.25 mile down to the old stone powerhouse at the base of the second tier. The power plant supplied much of the electricity to Wasco and Sher-man Counties from 1910 until the completion of The Dalles Dam in 1960 made it obsolete.

White River Falls

Continuing along the trail for another few hundred yards, through sage and juniper and past the old powerhouse, brings you to the broad, 25-foot-high punchbowl of Lower White River Falls.

Although the falls has been highly developed, it still remains very scenic. Photographers will easily be able to compose images with or without elements of the old power station. The area is relatively open, so use the early morning hours to avoid the harsh midday light.

112

DILLON FALLS

Location: Deschutes River State Recreation Area
Maps: USGS–Benham Falls
Stream: Deschutes River
Round Trip Hike Distance: 0.12 mile

Difficulty: Easy
Height: 20 feet
Volume: Large
Best Season: Spring, summer, fall, winter

SPECIAL NOTES: No fees or access permits are required.

DIRECTIONS: From Bend, follow Century Drive toward the Cascade Lakes Highway (US 372). After 6.5 miles, turn left onto FS 41 following the signs for the Deschutes River State Recreation Area. Follow FS 41 for 3 miles to FS 600 and turn left, following the signs to Dillon Falls 1 mile to its end at the trailhead.

THE FALLS: The short trail leads downstream from the parking area to several viewpoints along the rim of the gorge, which is lined with sagebrush and tall ponderosa pine. The waterfall itself is a 20-foot drop, followed by a series of large rapids. Here, like Benham Falls, the Deschutes River carved its way through an ancient lava dam created by the nearby Lava Butte cinder cone. Although there is no "grand view" of the falls, the setting and the view of the violent Deschutes is very scenic. The falls were named after homesteader Leander Dillon.

Like nearby Benham Falls, the best light for photography is in the early morning or late afternoon. Wide-angle lenses, a graduated neutral density filter, and polarizer are essential.

113

BENHAM FALLS

Location: Deschutes River State
Recreation Area
Maps: USGS–Benham Falls
Stream: Deschutes River
Round Trip Hike Distance:
0.25 mile

Difficulty: Easy
Height: 40 feet
Volume: Large
Best Season: Spring, summer, fall,
winter

SPECIAL NOTES: No fees or access permits are required. The trail is rough but still suitable for wheelchairs.

DIRECTIONS: From Bend follow Century Drive toward the Cascade Lakes Highway (US 372). After 6.5 miles turn left onto FS 41 following the signs for the Deschutes River State Recreation Area. Follow FS 41 for 4 miles to FS 400 and turn left, following the signs for another 2.5 miles to its end at the trailhead.

THE FALLS: From the parking area, a short dirt path leads down to a fenced viewpoint overlooking the falls. Here the Deschutes River drops 40 feet down a staircase-like section of the basalt lava gorge. Named for J. R. Benham, an early homesteader of the region, Benham Falls is the first of a series of three waterfalls on the Deschutes River as it passes through the Lava Butte Geological Area. About 7,000 years ago, a lava flow erupted from the nearby Lava Butte cinder cone. Lava poured from the cone and spilled into the Deschutes River, changing its course in some places and forming lava dams in others. Dillon Falls, Lava Island Falls, and Benham Falls are the remnants of these dams.

If you are photographing the falls, the best light is in the early morning or late afternoon. Wide-angle lenses, a graduated neutral density filter, and polarizer are essential.

114

TUMALO FALLS

Location: Deschutes National
Forest
Maps: USGS–Tumalo Falls
Stream: Tumalo Creek
Round Trip Hike Distance:
0.5–2.5 miles

Difficulty: Easy to moderate
Height: Tumalo Falls, 100 feet;
Middle Tumalo Falls, 65 feet
Volume: Large
Best Season: Spring, summer, fall,
winter

SPECIAL NOTES: A day-use fee or Northwest Forest Pass is required.

DIRECTIONS: From Bend, follow Franklin Avenue, which soon becomes Galveston Avenue and then Skyliner Drive, 11 miles west to FS 1828. Turn left onto the gravel FS 1828 and follow it 3 miles to the Tumalo Falls picnic area.

THE FALLS: From the picnic area, follow the well-graded trail upstream, to several viewpoints that look up the canyon to the falls. As you continue along the path, you will pass through vine maple and manzanita. In 1979, this was the scene of a forest fire that swept through the area. While a few ponderosa and lodgepole pine were spared, the scars of the fire remain in the form of tall, weathered snags.

After 0.25 mile, you reach the viewing platform perched on the edge of the cliff overlooking the 100-foot-high falls as it plunges onto the rocks below.

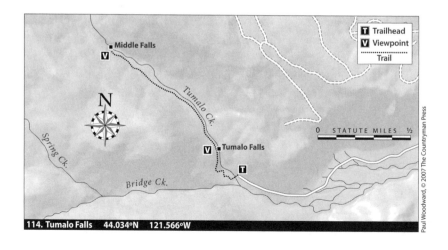

If you continue along the path, the forest soon begins to thicken with ponderosa pine and sagebrush, as here it escaped the brunt of the earlier fire. After 1.25 miles, you come to a viewpoint near the base of Middle Tumalo Falls. Totaling 65 feet, this two-tiered waterfall first slides 35 feet into a small plunge pool, and then plunges another 30 feet into a somewhat larger, rock-strewn plunge pool.

Both of the waterfalls face primarily south, so the best time of day to photograph is in the early morning hours. A warming filter and polarizer may be of use.

115

PAULINA CREEK FALLS

Location: Newberry National
Volcanic Monument
Maps: National Monument
brochure, USGS–Paulina Peak
Stream: Paulina Creek
Round Trip Hike Distance: 0.75
mile
Difficulty: Easy
Height: 60 feet
Volume: Medium
Best Season: Spring, summer, fall

SPECIAL NOTES: An National Park entrance fee is required for the monument.

DIRECTIONS: From Bend follow US 97 south 22 miles to FS 21, just 7 miles north of LaPine. Follow the Newberry National Volcanic Monument sign and turn left following FS 21 approximately 12 miles to the entrance of the national monument.

THE FALLS: The Newberry National Volcanic Monument was created in 1990, and offers a unique opportunity to view one of Oregon's youngest, and still active, volcanic regions. While only a stone's throw away from the Cascades, the Newberry Volcano is actually not a Cascades volcano, but rather a member of Oregon's High Lava Plains, which encompass much of the southeastern part of the state. In addition to the waterfall, the Newberry National Volcanic Monument offers camping, fishing, swimming, and several short hikes that will satisfy the geologist and naturalist, as well as the family looking for a weekend getaway.

Paulina Creek Falls and picnic area greet you on the left as you enter

Paulina Creek Falls

the national monument. This short 1.5-mile hike offers several views of the twin 60-foot waterfalls as Paulina Creek carves through the caldera wall on its journey to the Little Deschutes River.

The trail begins at the north end of the parking area. Turn left, following the wooded path down 0.5 mile to a small platform and a great view from below the falls. From here, retrace your steps to the picnic area, and another view of the falls from a fenced viewpoint on the rim.

Yet a third viewpoint lies across the creek, on the opposite side of the rim. To reach it, follow the trail upstream past the picnic area. The trail follows the creek for 0.5 mile, where it joins the resort road. Cross the bridge over Paulina Creek and turn right, to head down the service road and back along the opposite side of the creek. After 0.25 mile, you'll come to a fenced viewpoint along the rim. On your return trip, follow the short trail to the resort store for a cold drink before retracing your path back down to the picnic area.

A classic shield volcano, Newberry first erupted a little more than 1 million years ago. Approximately 500,000 years ago, major eruptions exhausted the magma beneath the volcano and, in a process similar to what occurred at Crater Lake, the 10,000 foot volcano collapsed in upon itself. Rain and snow filled the newly formed caldera to create a single lake, until the eruption of the Central Pumice Cone split the lake in two about 7,000 years ago. Paulina Lake takes its name from Chief Paulina of the Snake tribe.

116

CHUSH FALLS

Location: Three Sisters
Wilderness Area

Maps: USGS–Trout Creek Butte

Stream: Wychus Creek

Round Trip Hike Distance: 2

miles

Difficulty: Easy

Height: 50 feet

Volume: Large

Best Season: Spring, summer, fall

SPECIAL NOTES: A Northwest Forest Pass is required to park at the trailhead and is available at ranger stations and from many private vendors.

DIRECTIONS: From Sisters, follow Elm Street (which soon becomes FS 16) south for 8 miles to FS 1514 and turn right. Follow FS 1514 for 5 miles to FS 1514-600, located just prior to crossing Wychus Creek, and turn left, following the dirt road 2 miles to a junction. Turn left at the junction and follow the road another 0.5 mile to the trailhead.

THE FALLS: The well-maintained trail climbs moderately, through a mixed ponderosa pine and lodgepole pine forest, as it parallels the creek. After 1 mile, the trail arrives at a viewpoint on the rim of the canyon looking down on the 50-foot-high waterfall. This classic fan, surrounded by tall pines, virtually explodes over a basalt escarpment and onto moss-covered rocks and snags. A short, steep trail leads from the viewpoint down to the best views of the falls at its base. However, be prepared to get wet, since this waterfall kicks up a lot of spray.

The falls face northeast, and photographers will want to arrive early. A wide-angle lens, polarizer, and graduated neutral density filter will also be of use. Spray at the base of the falls will also be a concern and some form of protection is recommended.

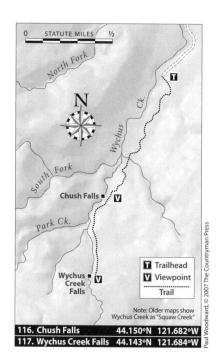

| 116. Chush Falls | 44.150°N 121.682°W |
| 117. Wychus Creek Falls | 44.143°N 121.684°W |

Paul Woodward, © 2007 The Countryman Press

117

WYCHUS CREEK FALLS

Location: Three Sisters
Wilderness Area
Maps: USGS–Trout Creek Butte
Stream: Wychus Creek
Round Trip Hike Distance: 3 miles

Difficulty: Easy
Height: 200 feet
Volume: Medium
Best Season: Spring, summer, fall

SPECIAL NOTES: A Northwest Forest Pass is required to park at the trailhead and is available at ranger stations and many private vendors.

DIRECTIONS: From Sisters, follow Elm Street (which soon becomes FS 16) south for 8 miles to FS 1514 and turn right. Follow FS 1514 for 5 miles to FS 1514-600 located just prior to crossing Wychus Creek, and turn left, following the dirt road 2 miles to a junction. Turn left at the junction, and follow the road another 0.5 mile to the trailhead.

THE FALLS: The well-maintained trail climbs moderately through a mixed ponderosa pine–lodgepole pine forest as it parallels the creek. After 1 mile, the trail arrives at a viewpoint on the rim of the canyon overlooking Chush Falls. From here the official maintained trail ends; however, a well-worn unofficial trail continues, and after 0.25 mile it encounters The Cascades. The 30-foot-high waterfall take a rough curtain form as it drops over the red lava rock common in the area.

The trail provides glimpses of the Wychus Creek Falls through the trees as it tumbles down the bluff just ahead. Just 0.25 mile past The Cascades, the trail more or less ends at the base of the 200-foot-high cataract. Here Wychus Creek slides down the first third of the falls before cascading the remaining 130 feet onto the rocks below.

The area is exceptionally scenic and photographers will want to bring the majority of their equipment. The open nature of the pine forest and the red hues of the iron-rich basalts and rhyolite are especially picturesque in the warm light around sunrise and sunset.

118

WIZARD FALLS

Location: Deschutes National Forest
Maps: USGS–Black Butte
Stream: Metolius River
Round Trip Hike Distance: At roadside

Difficulty: Easy
Height: 3 feet
Volume: Large
Best Season: Spring, summer, fall, winter

SPECIAL NOTES: No fees or access passes are required. On weekends during the summer months, the area around the fish hatchery and springs can become fairly crowded.

DIRECTIONS: From Sisters, drive west on US 20 nine miles to FS 14 (Camp Sherman). Follow FS 14 approximately 11 miles to the Wizard Falls Fish Hatchery on the left.

THE FALLS: The Wizard Falls Fish Hatchery was opened in 1948.

Wizard Falls

Nestled under the large ponderosa pine and cedar trees are various hold-ing tanks, which contain as many as 3 million rainbow, brook, and brown trout, as well as kokanee and Atlantic salmon. A large holding pond at the